Moonology™
Diary 2023

Yasmin Boland

HAY HOUSE
Carlsbad, California • New York City
London • Sydney • New Delhi

This diary belongs to

Vanessa Lake

Published in the United Kingdom by:
Hay House UK Ltd, The Sixth Floor, Watson House,
54 Baker Street, London W1U 7BU
Tel: +44 (0)20 3927 7290; Fax: +44 (0)20 3927 7291; www.hayhouse.co.uk

Published in the United States of America by:
Hay House Inc., PO Box 5100, Carlsbad, CA 92018-5100
Tel: (1) 760 431 7695 or (800) 654 5126
Fax: (1) 760 431 6948 or (800) 650 5115; www.hayhouse.com

Published in Australia by:
Hay House Australia Pty. Ltd, 18/36 Ralph St, Alexandria NSW 2015
Tel: (61) 2 9669 4299; Fax: (61) 2 9669 4144; www.hayhouse.com.au

Published in India by:
Hay House Publishers India, Muskaan Complex, Plot No.3, B-2,
Vasant Kunj, New Delhi 110 070
Tel: (91) 11 4176 1620; Fax: (91) 11 4176 1630; www.hayhouse.co.in

A catalogue record for this book is available from the British Library.

ISBN: 978-1-78817-658-3

Interior images: Endpapers, vi, 9: Shutterstock; ii, 13, 22, 38: DesignWorkBoutique/ Etsy; 46, 56, 66, 76, 86, 94, 104, 112, 122, 130, 148, 160, 168, 178, 186, 194, 204, 212, 222, 230, 250, 260, 268: Lana Elanor/creative market; all other images Alisovna/ creative market

Printed and bound in Italy by Graphicom

Contents

So What's Up for 2023?

If you want a key phrase for the astrology of 2023, here it is: humanity is transforming! That might sound a little fanciful or pie-in-the-sky, but it's really not stretching the astrological truth at all. This year, the planets really do support us all – the whole of humanity – in transforming our lives, perhaps forcing us to make those changes we promised ourselves we'd make back in 2020, 2021 and 2022.

It's a year to throw out the dead wood from our lives, to look at win-win solutions for the whole world, to move away from individual selfishness and to think about the greater good. In everything we do, as a species, we must start to look for win-win outcomes. Once again, you might think this sound like 'too much', but wait and see. It really is the promise of this year's energies.

The Big Astro-Headlines of 2023

Here is a quick summary of the astrology that we're going to be dealing with in 2023. Remember, the astrology of the year acts as a kind of a backdrop as we do our Moon work. We can't really *not* take it into account. Also note that all the main outer planetary action takes place between January and June. The energies will be rising just beforehand and fading out afterwards.

Date	Astrological event	What it means for you
7 March 2023	Saturn moves into Pisces	Get disciplined in your spiritual practices
12 March 2023	Jupiter meets Chiron	There is so much healing in the air
23 March 2023	Pluto moves into Aquarius	Humanity can transform
16 May 2023	Jupiter moves into Taurus	Very promising for the planet's finances
18 May 2023	Jupiter clashes with Pluto	Don't pay the ferryman
11 June 2023	Pluto moves into Capricorn	Last chances to implement the lessons from 2008 through to the present day
19 June 2023	Jupiter harmonizes with Saturn	Hard work leads to growth

Here's a bit more detail about each of these power dates:

7 March: the massive planet Saturn changes signs and moves into Pisces. It's always big news when Saturn changes signs, which it only does about once every two years. Saturn is the planet of karma and lessons, so whenever he changes signs, it's as though we start to play out – and get lessons for – a whole new part of our life. See page 85 to discover more about how this move will be playing out for you. Saturn was last in Pisces from late January 1994 through to early April 1996.

12 March: the planet of good luck and good things, Jupiter, meets the planetoid of healing, Chiron. Not all astrologers work with Chiron's medicine, but in the interests of keeping things balanced as I outline the energies of the year ahead, this is a really positive one. There is a lot of room for healing, if we play our Chiron cards right.

23 March: this is probably the biggest astrological event of the year. The planet of power and passion, Pluto, is changing signs and moving into the sign of Aquarius. To put this in perspective, the last transit of Pluto in Aquarius began in 1778. One of Pluto's symbols is the crucible. It's heat and volcanoes and transformation. It's intangible and psychological and all about the cycle of life, death and rebirth. That's what the world – humanity – has in store this year.

Why humanity? Because Pluto will be exploding in Aquarius, which is the sign of humanity. Since 2008, Pluto has been in Capricorn – the sign of, among other things, business – and indeed we've seen businesses, and even the way we do business, transformed since 2008.

So let's hope Pluto in Aquarius will be about burning away the past. It's time to detox (a very Pluto word) humanity. It's purge-or-perish time (purge and perish are also Pluto words). I told you it's intense! On a personal level, the best question to ask yourself as you read this is: *where in my life do I need a detox?* Note that Pluto will be in and out of Capricorn and Aquarius between now and November 2024. But this is the beginning of that phase. See pages 93–94 to discover more about what this means for you.

16 May: this date sees the lucky planet Jupiter moving into the sign of Taurus. This is good news! Taurus is the sign associated with sensuality and all things natural, as well as with money and Wall Street. Jupiter is the good luck planet that amplifies. Having Jupiter in Taurus definitely sounds like one of the most assuredly positive aspects of the first half of 2023. Whereas the past few years saw many people and businesses struggle, now there is a positive outlook.

18 May: unfortunately, the first thing Jupiter does as it moves into Taurus is clash with Pluto. Hopefully this just takes us one step further away from the pandemic. Why? Because the pandemic more or less took over the world under a Jupiter–Pluto meeting in 2020.

11 June: Pluto is retrograding back into Capricorn. This will be Pluto's last hurrah in this sign, a cycle which started in 2008. That cycle has been about stripping the business world back, cutting fat, changing the way governments work and increasing the emphasis on professional ethics. Pluto will remain back in Capricorn for this final fling until January 2024.

19 June: just when you thought it was going to be all dramas and challenges in 2023, along comes a lovely and harmonious alignment between Jupiter and Saturn. This is the last major planetary alignment of the outer planets (the slower-moving Jupiter, Saturn, Uranus, Neptune and Pluto) and a rather positive note to end on. When the outer planets are aligning, life can often be very challenging, but the absence of any major alignments in the second half of 2023 suggests we should all be a little less under stress. But it's a bit weird, too, not to have any major alignments until April 2023 – in other words, for 10 months! The good news is that, if you imagine astrology as the music of the spheres, the hum in the background between various outer planets during that time is harmonious.

Planetary Retrogrades for the Year

Mercury retrograde

The year 2023 begins and ends with a Mercury retrograde cycle. This is the time to double-check everything and an opportunity for second chances. It's a time to rethink, revisit and review, and also when communication can go very haywire! I have some Mercury retrograde freebies at www.moonmessages.com/mercuryfree.

Date	Retrograde cycle
18 January 2023	Mercury retrograde in Capricorn ends
21 April 2023	Mercury retrograde in Taurus begins
15 May 2023	Mercury retrograde in Taurus ends
23 August 2023	Mercury retrograde in Virgo begins
15 September 2023	Mercury retrograde in Virgo ends
13 December 2023	Mercury retrograde in Capricorn begins

Venus retrograde

Exceptionally, Venus, the planet of love and abundance, goes retrograde in 2023. This only happens about once in every 18 months. It's a time when you can feel a little detached from your partner, but also a good time to re-evaluate who really matters to you and what you really value.

Date	Retrograde cycle
23 July 2023	Venus goes retrograde in Leo
4 September 2023	Venus in Leo retrograde ends

Mars retrograde

Until 12 January 2023, Mars is retrograde, which means it's a time when Mars' fiery energy turns in on itself. The plus side of this is that people put down their guns, so to speak; however, as Mars is the fire in the belly of the zodiac, it can also be a time when motivation is lacking.

The outer planets in retrograde

Jupiter, Saturn, Uranus, Neptune and Pluto spend a good part of every year retrograde. Here are the dates for 2023:

Date	Retrograde cycle	What it means for you
22 January 2023	Uranus retrograde in Taurus ends	Every time the Moon or one of the planets triggers Uranus, we'll feel just that little bit of extra chaos. Sometimes it shunts us forwards nicely and sometimes it jars.

Date	Retrograde cycle	What it means for you
1 May 2023	Pluto goes retrograde in Aquarius (until 11 October 2023)	Every time the Moon or one of the planets triggers Pluto, we get a chance to drop the power struggle and look for a win-win outcome.
17 June 2023	Saturn goes retrograde in Pisces (until 4 November 2023)	Every time the Moon or one of the planets triggers Saturn, we get a Saturnian vibe — could be tough lessons we need, could be a chance to get serious or consolidate.
30 June 2023	Neptune goes retrograde in Pisces (until 6 December 2023)	Every time the Moon or one of the planets triggers Neptune, for better or worse, we can feel anything from disappointed (if there's a clash) or inspired (if it's a harmonious alignment).
23 July 2023	Chiron goes retrograde in Aries (until 27 December 2023)	Every time the Moon or one of the planets triggers Chiron, we get a chance to heal a wound — even wounds that we feared would never heal.
29 August 2023	Uranus goes retrograde in Taurus (this lasts into 2024)	See entry for 22 January
4 September 2023	Jupiter goes retrograde in Taurus (until 24 December 2023)	Every time the Moon or one of the planets triggers Jupiter, we get a shot of excess, or maybe a quick hit of good luck!

Date	Retrograde cycle	What it means for you
11 October 2023	Pluto retrograde in Capricorn ends	See entry for 1 May
4 November 2023	Saturn retrograde in Pisces ends	See entry for 17 June
6 December 2023	Neptune retrograde in Pisces ends	See entry for 30 June
27 December 2023	Chiron retrograde in Aries ends	See entry for 23 July
31 December 2023	Jupiter retrograde in Taurus ends	See entry for 4 September

What Does It All Mean?

So, is 2023 going to be another dreadful year? Chances are: no. I'll be completely transparent: at the time of writing (in June 2021), we're all crossing our fingers and toes and everything else, hoping that by 2023 the pandemic will be just a fading memory. And it should be. Hopefully we'll all be in the process of rebuilding our lives. Hopefully we can all just breathe out and move on. But could there be some echoes of the pandemic in 2023? Oh yes, there could.

The good news for the planet is the move of Saturn into Pisces. Why is this good news? Saturn is the planet of confinement and limitations. So what did we see when Saturn was in the sign of Aquarius – the sign of humanity, remember – most recently? I suspect you already know the answer to that: humanity was in lockdown. So now, as Saturn finally moves out of Aquarius and into Pisces, those days should become a fading memory.

So what will Saturn be influencing instead in Pisces? My hope is that something I've sensed developing for a long time will materialize; namely that it becomes really normal for cosmic types (healers, magical practitioners, shamans, astrologers and so on – all very Piscean) to do regular work (Saturn is all about regular work). Maybe this is the year it becomes normal to have an empath or psychic on speed dial so you can ask them what's coming up for you, your company or even the stock market. And because every event is said to have an equal and opposite reaction, it could also be the year that the powers that be (read: government) start to clamp down on people making false claims about what they can and can't do in terms of healing and so on. Both would seem to be a good thing.

Saturn is also the planet of learning, and in Pisces it's safe bet that we can learn more about the wonders of the numinous. Think: proper studies into the benefits of meditation and maybe even decent investigations into the mind–body connection.

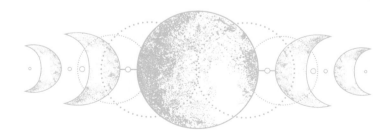

2023 is my year of transformation and abundance!*

* We chose this mantra because, as you'll read, there is extra transformation and abundance in the air this year! Say this mantra every day — a few times a day — until you start to feel it in your body. Write it down. Make it your motto.

The Phases of the Moon

At this point, you may be thinking: *hang on, I thought I bought a Moonology diary, what's all this about astrology?* The planetary activity for the year ahead is the background against which all the New and Full Moons and eclipses will take place, so we have to take the bigger planetary picture into account if we're to assess the year ahead in any meaningful way. Think of the astrology as the small hand on an old-fashioned watch and the Moonology as the big hand.

The Moon goes through the same nine phases, in the same order, every single month: astrologically speaking, we get the New Moon, the Waxing Crescent Moon, the First Quarter Moon, the Gibbous Moon, the Full Moon, the Disseminating Moon, the Third Quarter Moon and the Balsamic Moon. As well, it's not strictly astrology but I also like to work with the Dark Moon, which comes at the very end of the Balsamic Moon, just before it turns into the New Moon.

Speaking broadly, this table explains what each of the phases is good for:

Symbol	Moon phase	What it means for you
	New Moon	Time to set intentions, not in an airy-fairy way, but really committing.
	Waxing Crescent Moon	Act on your intentions. It's pedal-to-the-metal time.
	First Quarter Moon	Challenges arise, all the better for you to recommit to your dreams.
	Gibbous Moon	This Moon is stuffed full of emotions, dreams and wishes – and you might feel a bit that way too!
	Full Moon	Emotional explosions are possible – you also see whether your dreams are manifesting.
	Disseminating Moon	A time to process all you've been through, and to start letting go of anything you need to release.
	Third Quarter Moon	Allow what didn't work to fall away, so you're unencumbered.
	Balsamic Moon	A soulful time with powerful healing vibes. Make peace with life.
	Dark Moon	When everything that's gone before can simply crumble away so that you can enter the New Moon phrase fresh.

In the southern hemisphere, the Moon appears the other way up compared with the northern hemisphere. This is simply due to your orientation. Imagine if the Moon orbited in the same plane as the equator, for example. If you're in the northern hemisphere, the equator is to your south, so the Moon will always appear in the southern sky. The reverse is true in the southern hemisphere: the Moon will appear in the northern sky. So, what you see in the northern hemisphere and southern hemisphere are mirror images of each other. With regard to the diagrams in this book, if you're in the southern hemisphere, you simply need to flip the moon symbols to relate them to your own night sky.

The Moonology of 2023

Naturally, we'll be working with the Moon this year, using the New Moon to set intentions and the Full Moon to do our release work. What a lot of people don't realize when they first start to work with the Moon is that each phase has its own meaning.

The New and Full Moons of 2023

There will be 25 New and Full Moons this year; 12 New Moons and 13 Full Moons. Notably, we get two New Moons in Aries, which is super-interesting, since the New Moon in the first sign of the zodiac, Aries, marks the astrological New Year. So you could say that we have two astrological New Years this year – three if you count the one on 1 January! Hopefully this translates as chance after chance for the world to start over. Note that the second of the two New Moons in Aries is an eclipse, which super-charges this situation.

As you'd expect, every month has at least one Full Moon (except for about once every 20 years in February!), but August has two (based on UK time). That makes the Full Moon in Pisces on 31 August a Blue Full Moon. While there is no astrological meaning to this *per se*, it's fun to note. Also, if you need to do something super-special and one-off, then choosing to do it symbolically at the time of the Blue Full Moon can surely only help! Remember too that, as we do Full Moon Forgiveness and Questions to Ask work every Full Moon, it means August brings double the opportunity for that (and double the chances of the heightened emotions that the Full Moon brings with it too!).

Other fun things to note, though again they're not really astrological (they're more astronomical), are the Supermoons and other special Moons for the year ahead. A Supermoon is a New or Full Moon that closely coincides with the Moon's closest point to Earth in her monthly orbit. A Super Full Moon will look up to 14 per cent larger and 30 per cent brighter than a Full Moon. There are between four and six Supermoons a year. Here are the dates (GMT) on which Supermoons and special Moons fall in the year ahead:

- 21 January: Super New Moon

- 20 February: Super New Moon

- 19 May: Black New Moon (the third New Moon in a season with four New Moons)

- 1 August: Super Full Moon

- 31 August: Blue Super Full Moon (the second Full Moon in a single calendar month)

The 2023 Eclipses

This year there will be just four eclipses (the minimum number of eclipses we can have in any one year is four; the maximum is seven).

Astrologically speaking, eclipses occur when the Sun and the Moon meet up in a New or Full Moon (so either on the same zodiac point or exactly opposite respectively) within 19 degrees of the so-called lunar nodes. The nodes are actually points in the sky where the Moon's orbital path crosses the ecliptic, the Sun's (apparent) yearly path on the celestial sphere.

Chronologically, the eclipses this year are taking place in the signs of Aries, Scorpio, Libra and Taurus. Here are the dates – you can find out more about the 'flavour' of each eclipse later in the diary:

- 20 April: New Moon eclipse in Aries

- 5 May: Full Moon eclipse in Scorpio

- 14 October: New Moon eclipse in Libra

- 28 October: Full Moon eclipse in Taurus

Working with the Energies throughout the Year

Now that you have an idea of what's ahead, I hope you'll use this diary to stay mindful of where we are energetically at any time. It'll change your life to become aware of the New and Full Moons, just for a start:

- Knowing it's a New Moon means recognizing that it's time to make sure you're clear about your desires and to send your wishes out to the Universe.

- Knowing that we're in a Waxing Cycle (from New to Full Moon) means understanding that it's time to go hard on achieving your goals.

- Knowing it's a Full Moon means realizing that it's time to surrender your wishes to the part of you that's Divine and connected to all life everywhere. Then see where that leaves you and what comes back to you after you surrender.

- Knowing that we're in a Waning Cycle (from Full Moon back to New) means acknowledging that this is the right moment for some downtime.

- Knowing it's a First or Third Quarter Moon means being aware that it's the right time to note down what you're grateful for. Doing this will really boost your manifesting because the more we appreciate the good in our lives, the more good we attract.

I do Facebook and Instagram lives for every New and Full Moon. I do these as much for myself as for the thousands of people who tune in either live or for the replay. It's very easy to have all these ideas about working with the Moon in your head as a sort of abstract concept, but I find that doing the rituals helps me to ground the ideas and make them real. People love them and I invite you to attend (for free!) at www.moonmessages.com/fbevents.

Manifesting with the New and Full Moons

I personally believe that one of the things we're here on Earth to learn is how to manifest. Sure, there's a school of thought that tells us just to surrender everything to the Divine, but I don't believe that's what we're meant to do.

I believe that we're meant to send our wishes out to the Universe at the New Moon and *then* to surrender at Full Moon, on the basis that maybe we have something to learn about life based on what it is we're wishing for and what is manifesting.

The New Moon and the Law of Attraction

If you've studied manifesting for any period of time, you'll already know that one of the biggest hurdles to overcome is lack of clarity about your goals. As they say, you can't get what you want until you know what you want. The New Moon, then, is the perfect time to work with the law of attraction every month, because it's the perfect time to get really clear about your desires.

As you may know, the New Moon was traditionally the time when magical women held rituals and sent their wishes out to the Universe. In the olden days, of course, this was in the form of spells. Hundreds of years of negative propaganda from the patriarchy about women doing this has meant that, these days, many of us will recoil at the mention of the word 'spells'. We've been taught that manifesting is somehow bad, that we shouldn't let the Universe decide what we want, that it's not wise for us to try to bend reality. Because of the dreadful persecution of women who used their natural powers, our DNA is pretty much hardwired to avoid doing anything that could lead to us being persecuted ourselves.

I'd argue that this is all a throwback to the so-called Burning Times. Those were the horrific days when an untold number of women were murdered for doing the magical work we're once again doing today. In case you don't know what I'm referring to here, I'd urge you to Google 'the Burning Times'. Those were the bad old days, when women were literally burned at the stake, hanged or drowned for using their innate magical powers. As a result of such persecution, we stopped doing it, for the most part. Women lost touch with their magical powers and stopped working with the Moon. But not all of them. Some women kept the tradition alive, continuing to make their magic by the light of the Moon and Her lunar phases.

Now as the Divine Feminine starts to re-emerge, women are once again making magic, and this time it's hopefully without fear. You don't have to call yourself a witch to make magic, by the way (I don't)!

There have been many teachers along my path, but here I want to acknowledge the amazing Sonia Choquette, who is a fellow Hay House author. I got to know Sonia a little bit a couple of years ago, when she was living in Paris and I was a regular visitor (as my husband is Parisian).

Sonia and I had some amazing discussions (before the pandemic intervened and stopped my trips to Paris). Perhaps the most amazing one was when she told me she believes Earth is a school of manifestation and that we actually come here to learn how to manifest. She also pointed out to me why it makes perfect sense that I've always done my manifesting with the Moon. She reminded me that, of course, the Moon in astrology is all about feelings (as I well knew). And how do we manifest? I also knew this because of reading Abraham-Hicks for so long – we manifest with our feelings! So in fact, the Moon is the perfect conduit for our manifesting.

In that one conversation Sonia took all the pieces of my jigsaw and put them together for me in a way I'd never thought of. My mind exploded! I hope this makes as much sense to you now as it did to me then.

Full Moon Forgiveness and Questions to Ask

We do Full Moon Forgiveness and Questions to Ask work to clear the way for our New Moon intention-setting. Doing this really boosts our manifesting, because the more we appreciate the good in our lives, the more good we attract. This is the law of attraction. You'll learn more about this as the year and the diary unfold.

In the meantime, here is the super-powerful 'Formula for Forgiveness and Karma Release' from my book *Moonology*™, where it appeared with the kind permission of Catherine Ponder (who let me tweak her version just a little!):

> '*Under the glorious Full Moon, I forgive everything, everyone, every experience, every memory of the past or present that needs forgiveness. I forgive positively everyone. I also forgive myself for past mistakes. The Universe is love, and I am forgiven and governed by love alone. Love is now adjusting my life. Realizing this, I abide in peace.*
>
> '*I bring love and healing to all my thoughts, beliefs and relationships. I learn my lessons and move on. I call on my soul fragments to be cleansed by the Full Moon and I call on them to rejoin me. I send love to myself and everyone I know, and everyone who knows me, in all directions of time. Under this glorious Full Moon, I am healed. My life is healed. And so it is. So be it.*'

Forgiveness, as you'll come to see during this year, really is the key to manifesting. Refer back to this formula at each Full Moon and repeat it with all your heart!

The Astro-Quarters of the Year

You might have heard of the Wheel of the Year, but did you know there is also a sort of Astrological Wheel of the Year? It's marked out by the moves of the Sun into Aries, Cancer, Libra and Capricorn, which are significant events astrologically speaking. These moves happen around the same time each year. Here are the dates for 2023:

- 20 March: the Sun moves into Aries (21 March Down Under)

- 21 June: the Sun moves into Cancer

- 23 September: the Sun moves into Libra

- 22 December: the Sun moves into Capricorn

They are known as 'ingresses' or 'Cardinal ingresses'. In astrology, an ingress is when a planet moves into a sign. The word Cardinal refers to the four so-called Cardinal signs of Aries, Cancer, Libra and Capricorn. These are dynamic signs known for their leadership ability. (Remember, we all have all 12 signs in our chart!) On each Cardinal ingress, check into the Diary Bonuses area at www.moonmessages.com/diarybonuses2023 for your quarterly 'Reflect and Review' worksheet.

So the Cardinal ingresses are when the Sun moves into one of the four Cardinal signs. Not long after the ingress, we'll get the New Moon in whichever sign the Sun has moved into.

Working with the Houses

On each of the New and Full Moon pages of this diary you'll find a section called 'How to Work with This Moon'. Each New and Full Moon takes place in one part of your chart, which is more or less a map of the skies at the moment were born, set for the place you were born. Astrologers divide this chart into 12 sections called Houses – and the Houses cover every part of your life, from your home and family to career and identity. So for example, your 4th House is about home and family, broadly speaking; your 7th House is about love and relationships; your 10th House is about career. On the following pages you'll discover more info about which part of your life is ruled by each House.

A New Moon activates beginnings, the chance to start over, a new burst of energy or a very good moment to make wishes in the part (House) of your chart where the New Moon is taking place. The Full Moons indicate climaxes and conclusions, that it may be time to turn a corner or that there is a tug of war and a need for balance in the part of your life indicated by where in your chart (which House) the Full Moon is taking place.

To know which House is being activated for you at each New and Full Moon, and hence where the energy of that Moon is for you, you can use your Star sign or your Rising sign, but your Rising sign is far more accurate.

Your Star sign is what astrologers call your Sun sign – it's where the Sun was when you were born. For example, if you were born when the Sun was in Gemini, then you 'are' a Gemini, and every person born at the same moment in time as you, anywhere in the world, will have the same Star sign.

Your Rising sign, however, is far more personal; it's the most personal point on your chart because it's dictated not just by your date and time of birth, but also by your place of birth. The Rising sign is the constellation of the zodiac that was coming up over the Eastern horizon at the moment you were born. So, while two people born at the exact moment in time in, say, Los Angeles and London will have all the *planets* in the same place, their Rising signs will be different. The Rising sign is important because it dictates the way your chart is laid out. Without wanting to get too complicated (I have a book called *Astrology Made Easy* if you want to dig deeper!), in a nutshell, when you use the 'How to Work with This Moon' sections in this diary, use your Rising sign to find out where the New or Full Moon is communing with your chart in the most personal and accurate way.

1. If you don't know your Rising Sign, go to www.moonmessages. com/freechart to find out.

2. When there is a New or Full Moon, check the section marked 'How to Work with This Moon'.

3. Look at your Rising Sign: which House is mentioned?

4. Look at 'A Quick Guide to the Houses' below to see which House on your chart is being activated.

5. If it's a New Moon, expect a new start; if it's a Full Moon, expect a turning point.

A Quick Guide to the Houses

The 1st House: your appearance and image; self-identity; how you come across to others.

The 2nd House: cash, property and possessions; values, including how you value yourself.

The 3rd House: communication; siblings; neighbours; quick trips; early education.

The 4th House: home and family; all things domestic; where you belong; your past.

The 5th House: romance; creativity; kids (your own or someone else's); pursuit of pleasure; love affairs.

The 6th House; daily routines, including at work; your health; duty.

The 7th House: your lovers, your spouse, and your ex; open enemies; any sort of partner, including business partners; cooperation and competition.

The 8th House: joint finances; credit cards; debts; sex; anything you consider taboo; inheritance; transformation.

The 9th House: study; travel; the Great Cosmic Quest; the Internet; higher learning; religion; big dreams.

The 10th House: your career and ambitions; how you make your mark on the world; what you're known for; reputation.

The 11th House: friends; networks; social circles; what you're wishing for.

The 12th House: the deepest, darkest, most sensitive part of your chart – your fears; your spirituality; self-undoing; withdrawal; dreams.

A question I'm often asked when readers get this information is: 'Should I make my wishes depending on which part of my chart is being activated?' The answer is yes, if you want to, but otherwise just make the wishes you have in your heart, and keep in mind where the lunation is communing with you.

The New Moon through the Houses

The 1st House

The New Moon is taking place in your 1st House this month, which is big news. It offers you the chance to start again in any part of your life in which you know that's needed. If you're really happy with the way things are going then consider an energy recharge to help propel you through the coming 12 months. If you want to change the way others see you, the next four weeks are the time to work on that.

The 2nd House

A New Moon in your 2nd House is all about cash, property and possessions. If you want changes in any of these aspects of your life, this New Moon is the ideal time to start to make them. Money is energy and it responds quite quickly to our thoughts of abundance.

If you've been thinking negatively about money, use this New Moon as a marker and decide to turn around your thoughts and expectations about it.

The 3rd House

When it comes to getting what we want, it's great to visualize and write wish lists, but also to communicate to others what we want. This invokes the law of attraction because speaking our desires means we need to have some conviction that we can get what we want. The New Moon this month in your Communication Zone brings energy galore for communication. What do you want? Who can help you? Just ask.

The 4th House

Your home life, your personal life, your domestic life, your past, your family, the people who feel like family and your actual home – all these parts of your life are up for renewal now as this month's New Moon focuses its energy on your 4th House. If you haven't been getting on well at home or with your family, this is the ideal time to sort things out. If you want to move, sell or buy, it's all possible.

The 5th House

Welcome to the House of Fun! Have you been having a bit of that lately? If not, then the skies are strongly suggesting that it's time to get out and do a little bit of what you fancy. Could you use a restart in terms of romance, creativity or kids? Identify which one(s) you want to work on and draw up an action plan. What could you do to inch closer to what you want? Remember, the law of attraction means we can't get what we want until we know what we want.

The 6th House

In one way, this is a dull and tedious House because it's the part of your chart that's all about your daily routines – not exactly riveting. However, this is also the part of your chart where you get a chance to tweak your schedules and routines so that, at the very least, your daily life runs in a way that pleases you. If minor changes are needed in these areas, this is a great month to put them in place.

The 7th House

How's your love life? There's a New Moon in your Love Zone this month, which means you're getting the chance to reinvigorate your love life. If you're single, this is the perfect time to move on from old loves, old dreams and any old heartaches. If you're attached, you're probably aware of the importance of keeping your relationship fresh – and this New Moon brings in fresh energy and a chance to think about some of the things you and your partner can do this month.

The 8th House

You have the New Moon in your 8th House this month. That means it's firing up the part of your chart that deals with sex and money. If your love life is dull, do whatever it takes to rev things up. If you've been inhibited, try something new. Go as far as you feel comfortable. Moneywise, it's all about where your money is involved with someone else, so you have a chance for a restart in terms of your income or salary; plus, it's a very good time to set up a debt-repayment plan.

The 9th House

This part of your chart is related to study, travel and adventure. There's a rush of new energy in these areas of your life, so if you have plans for them, ask for the skies' support. This part of your chart is about seeing The Big Picture of your life. It's about higher learning and self-improvement. This is the month to open your eyes to the big wide world, rather than fretting about all the little details on the home front.

The 10th House

This month's New Moon is flooding your professional or student life with potential and ambition. If you're already on the right path in your working life, then this lunation can really amp things up. However, if you're struggling professionally and not quite sure where to turn, use this New Moon as a marker. Over the coming four weeks, really put yourself out there – research your job market and talk to experts who can help you get where you want to be.

The 11th House

The New Moon in your 11th House relates to your friends and the things you're wishing for. Having the New Moon here is very auspicious for two reasons: firstly, it means that, over the coming four weeks, you're in a cycle when you can meet new people, so be open to having new friends in your life; secondly, it's a hugely important time for manifesting.

The 12th House

You're in a slightly strange cycle – can you feel it? This month, the New Moon is taking place in the part of your chart where you keep

All Matters Hidden and Spiritual. This can be a time when you just want to withdraw from the world, or, if you're on a spiritual path, you might want to take time out from the madness to meditate. Know that the Universe will deliver the messages you need to hear.

The Full Moon through the Houses

The 1st House

It's all very well being focused on someone else, but once a year the Full Moon reminds you that you also need to focus on yourself: and that time is now. Many of us are givers rather than takers, and this can mess with the flow in our lives. So, this month remember to say yes when people offer help. You could feel emotional during this cycle, but a lot of the 'stuff' that's coming up needs to be dealt with!

The 2nd House

Balance is required between what you do for yourself financially and what you do for others. Consider your income and your debts; your self-worth and what others pay you, which is usually based on what you ask for. If you're about to make a major purchase, you're doing it at the right time. If you've been letting someone control you because they have financial power over you, this is your chance to break free.

The 3rd House

It's all very well dreaming of the Great Escape to a far-flung corner of the world or even the nearby countryside, but what about the details? This Full Moon is reminding you that things need to be taken care of close to home. It's also a reminder to express yourself. If you haven't been honest about how you feel, now is the time to start to say your piece. Dramas with siblings can be sorted now too.

The 4th House

Working like a dog to achieve your personal goals seems like a good thing, but there's a time and a place for everything. Right now, you're entering a cycle when you need to find a balance between your outer aims and your inner needs. Take a look at your family relationships and ascertain whether everything is running as smoothly as you'd like. If not, this is the time to pour some energy into that part of your life.

The 5th House

The Full Moon is taking place in your House of Self-Expression so there's a whole lot of emotion going on now. For some, it's all about pouring your heart out; for others, it's about the joy a child brings or pouring emotion into a creative project. And among all this, you need to find a balance between your Self and your friends. Don't neglect them totally! This is your challenge for the coming month.

The 6th House

If you're one of the lucky ones, this is the Full Moon when you see yourself for who you *really* are – your good points and your flaws – and you decide to do something about your flaws. This is all about the daily life you lead. Are you living healthily, exercising, and getting enough sleep? If not, then this Full Moon is your annual chance to start taking care of yourself – body, mind and spirit.

The 7th House

This Full Moon suggests it's time for you to step aside a little and invest some emotional energy in other people: your significant other, business partner or even an adversary. At the very least there needs to be a balance – it seems someone else needs your attention. The Full Moon can also bring closures, so if you're in a friendship or relationship that's ending, you can proceed in the knowledge that you're finishing things up at the right time, celestially speaking.

The 8th House

This Full Moon is all about finding a balance between give and take. If you know you've been doing too much of either, it's time to redress the balance. When you give too much but don't know how to take, how can the Universe send you an abundant stream of good things if you're not receiving them without a fight? Now is a good time to attend to practical financial matters, like paying off debts. It's also very good for investing some emotion in the boudoir.

The 9th House

Personal growth, religion, philosophy, publishing, the Internet, travel, and study – these are just some of the subjects looming large for you now as the Full Moon takes place in your 9th House. Be honest with yourself: have you been fussing too much over the details of your latest problems or tasks? If so, step back and look at the big picture of where you are and where you want to be. This is a great time to try something that's beyond your usual everyday realm.

The 10th House

If you've been hiding yourself away and generally keeping a low profile, watch out. The skies are suggesting loudly that it's time for you to step out of the shadows and back into the limelight. As tempting as it might be to slouch around at home, this Full Moon in your 10th House of Career is telling you it's time to invest some emotional energy in your professional life. If a work situation is coming to an end, something new will come in its place soon enough.

The 11th House

Of course, it's tempting for each of us to focus on our own pleasures. Life is for living and having fun, after all. However, this month's Full Moon in your 11th House is reminding you that you need to find a balance between indulging yourself and remembering that the people in your life also need some attention – from you. Whatever you do now for someone else, you'll get extra karmic brownie points. This also makes the coming month good for networking.

The 12th House

Life has probably felt very busy recently and no one can blame you for wanting to take some time out. The Full Moon in your 12th House is going to allow you to do just that. For many people, it comes at a time when they're feeling a bit down; however, you're probably just exhausted from the demands of daily life. Take some time out. If you know how to meditate or practise yoga, go for it. You need to strike a balance between working and time out.

What's Your Big, Beautiful Goal?

There's nothing like having one big goal for the year, and this diary is going to help you with that. So take a moment now to think about what you want to have achieved by the time the year is out and write it below.

My big, beautiful and audacious goal for 2023 is:

buy a house

Now come up with at least 3 solid reasons for this goal. It's really important to know your 'why' – come back to your why if ever you feel tired, lazy, discouraged, demotivated or just need a boost!

1. Because *My pets need more space*

2. Because *I want to connect to nature*

3. Because *I need peace my own energy not neighbours*

How do you plan to achieve your big, beautiful goal? Easy! Take it one day at a time, one month at a time. Use the space below to lay out the steps you need to achieve your goal. If you think your goal will just take, for example, three months, then set out the steps you'll take from January to March. You can come back and fill in subsequent months later. (I've also included quarterly 'Reflect and Review' exercises in the Diary Bonuses area to help you with this; visit www.moonmessages.com/diarybonuses2023.)

In January I will: exercise build strength

In February I will: look for be given house

In March I will: make physical move, invite parents

In April I will: connect w/ resources - mow, handyman

In May I will: garden landscape buy furniture memorial sale

In June I will: bon fire solstice ceremony house warming

In July I will: 4th sale furnishings.

In August I will:

In September I will: celebrate bday

In October I will: set up plow service

In November I will: host Thanksgiving w/ sis + parents

In December I will:

How to Use This Diary

Every month, I offer you a two-page overview of the energies of the month ahead, followed by detailed information about each New and Full Moon and the overall energies you can expect. You'll also find suggested exercises for each New and Full Moon, which have been created specifically with the energies of the particular lunation in mind.

There's also plenty of daily diary space for you to write in. One thing I've realized over the years of writing this diary is that everyone uses this space differently! Some use it to note their feelings on the day, some to mention what they're grateful for, some to note down their daily oracle or tarot-card draw and others to note down their appointments.

On these daily diary pages you'll see symbols to denote the Moon's phase and astrology symbols to denote which Star sign the Moon is in on any given day. When you see two astrology symbols, it means the Moon transitions from the first sign to the second on that day. These are the 12 Star signs and their symbols:

Aries	♈	Libra	♎
Taurus	♉	Scorpio	♏
Gemini	♊	Sagittarius	♐
Cancer	♋	Capricorn	♑
Leo	♌	Aquarius	♒
Virgo	♍	Pisces	♓

On the dates of the New and Full Moons, I've included the degrees at which each lunation occurs. If you think of the zodiac as a circle of 12 signs, each sign represents 30° (expressed as 0–29°) of the full 360° chart. Each degree is further divided into 60 minutes, which are expressed from 0–59. So, for instance, the notation 12°Cp20' means that the lunation occurs at 12° and 20 minutes in Capricorn.

The diary pages for each New and Full Moon also offer you affirmations. We have special permission to use these affirmations, which are from the founder of Hay House, Louise Hay. This is a big blessing for us all, so please read them, say them out loud and keep them in your heart!

At New Moon we give you space to write down your wishes and intentions. This is possibly the most powerful part of the diary if you're keen to put your manifesting skills to work. Writing down your wishes creates a special magic that thinking alone somehow can't reproduce. If, for any reason, you don't want to write down your wishes, use the prompts in the diary and speak your wishes into being instead.

At Full Moon, it's time to write your all-important Forgiveness and Release list – and burn it. Doing this release work at Full Moon is one of the most powerful activities you can do to boost your New Moon wishes because non-attachment is a super-important part of the manifesting process.

This year, for the first time, the diary includes 'Reflect and Review' sections at each of the Cardinal ingresses. These are housed in the Diary Bonuses area (visit www.moonmessages.com/diarybonuses2023). Not only are these a great point at which to take a breath and think about the past three months and the three months ahead, but they are also a great time to check in on the goals you set on pages 34–35 and at each previous ingress.

So it's time to dive in! Have an amazing 2023!

Yasmin

Weekly Diary

JANUARY

M	T	W	T	F	S	S
						1
2	3	4	5	6	7	8
9	10	11	12	13	14	15
16	17	18	19	20	21	22
23	24	25	26	27	28	29
30	31					

FEBRUARY

M	T	W	T	F	S	S
		1	2	3	4	5
6	7	8	9	10	11	12
13	14	15	16	17	18	19
20	21	22	23	24	25	26
27	28					

MARCH

M	T	W	T	F	S	S
		1	2	3	4	5
6	7	8	9	10	11	12
13	14	15	16	17	18	19
20	21	22	23	24	25	26
27	28	29	30	31		

APRIL

M	T	W	T	F	S	S
					1	2
3	4	5	6	7	8	9
10	11	12	13	14	15	16
17	18	19	20	21	22	23
24	25	26	27	28	29	30

MAY

M	T	W	T	F	S	S
1	2	3	4	5	6	7
8	9	10	11	12	13	14
15	16	17	18	19	20	21
22	23	24	25	26	27	28
29	30	31				

JUNE

M	T	W	T	F	S	S
			1	2	3	4
5	6	7	8	9	10	11
12	13	14	15	16	17	18
19	20	21	22	23	24	25
26	27	28	29	30		

JULY

M	T	W	T	F	S	S
					1	2
3	4	5	6	7	8	9
10	11	12	13	14	15	16
17	18	19	20	21	22	23
24	25	26	27	28	29	30
31						

AUGUST

M	T	W	T	F	S	S
	1	2	3	4	5	6
7	8	9	10	11	12	13
14	15	16	17	18	19	20
21	22	23	24	25	26	27
28	29	30	31			

SEPTEMBER

M	T	W	T	F	S	S
				1	2	3
4	5	6	7	8	9	10
11	12	13	14	15	16	17
18	19	20	21	22	23	24
25	26	27	28	29	30	

OCTOBER

M	T	W	T	F	S	S
						1
2	3	4	5	6	7	8
9	10	11	12	13	14	15
16	17	18	19	20	21	22
23	24	25	26	27	28	29
30	31					

NOVEMBER

M	T	W	T	F	S	S
		1	2	3	4	5
6	7	8	9	10	11	12
13	14	15	16	17	18	19
20	21	22	23	24	25	26
27	28	29	30			

DECEMBER

M	T	W	T	F	S	S
				1	2	3
4	5	6	7	8	9	10
11	12	13	14	15	16	17
18	19	20	21	22	23	24
25	26	27	28	29	30	31

January

Full Moon: 6/7 January
Third Quarter Moon: 15 January
New Moon: 21/22 January
First Quarter Moon: 28 January

So, here we are, at the start of another year. How are you feeling about life and what's in your heart? Are you the kind of person who likes to set New Year's resolutions and, if so, have you filled out the section (see pages 34–35) about your big, beautiful goal for the year ahead? If you don't like to set goals for yourself, I'd encourage you to ask yourself: why not? Are you worried about disappointing yourself? Here's the thing: if you do set some goals, you're far likelier to achieve them! So dare to have a go. As my mum always says, 'If you aim for the Moon, you might at least hit the top of a tree!'

January sees first a Full Moon and then a New Moon. Let go of anything which didn't work out for you last year at Full Moon. Then, at New Moon, you can really commit to your goals for the year ahead.

Something to note as we go through January is this: the year starts with the mind planet Mercury, and both the mind planet and Mars, the action planet, are retrograde. So it's a time to rest, rethink and review. Use the first couple of weeks to think about where you are in life and where you want to be. Gently ask yourself what you could have done better in 2022 and what you're going to improve on this year. Be kind to yourself, though – this isn't about beating yourself up! By the end of the month, both planets will have turned direct (ended their latest retrograde cycle), so go into the year gently and you'll be aligned with the energies.

This month I will:
❑ Rest
❑ Review 2022
❑ Make some plans for 2023

Full Moon
in Cancer

KEY WORDS AND IDEAS
FOR THIS LUNATION:

- Forgive
- Move on
- Make peace
- Say sorry

DATE AND TIME OF THIS MOON
London: 6 Jan, 23:07 | Sydney: 7 Jan, 10:07 | LA: 6 Jan, 15:07 | New York: 6 Jan, 18:07

The sign of Cancer is the most sentimental of signs. It's the part of you that reminisces and feels nostalgic. So take a fond backwards glance at whatever you're leaving behind you and consigning to the past. Note that the Full Moon in Cancer takes place when the Moon is in gentle Cancer and the Sun is on the opposite side of the skies, in super-rational, plan-loving Capricorn.

> Every Full Moon brings a tug of war, so make a plan for 2023 – and stick to it. Your challenge now is to find a balance between sentimentality and the reality of what you need to do or face.

This Full Moon is particularly well suited to that backwards glance, as it nudges right up to Mercury, which is retrograde. Use the energies to forgive and move on from anything and everything in your life that you need to release.

There are some very powerful energies around now, as the Full Moon is also activating Pluto, the planet that's all about eruptions and detoxing. You might be amazed by how powerful it is to start doing Full Moon Forgiveness, which is something I recommend that you commit to every single month.

Forgiving is about letting go and moving on. It means you accept the past and live in the present while looking to the future. It's one of the most powerful things you can do for yourself. We talk a lot about wishes and creating our own reality, but unless we slough off the past we're stuck there. Get it?

A Watery Farewell

Working with symbolism is one of the most powerful ways to create rituals. As you might know, in astrology every sign belongs to one of four elements: fire, earth, air or water. Cancer is a water sign, so this month, we're working with water. Simply fill a glass with water and speak into it all that you wish to leave behind in the past. Where forgiveness is needed, offer or ask for it. Slowly pour the water away, and as you do say something along the lines of 'So long, goodbye, and thank you for the lessons....'

How to Work with This Moon

To discover where the energy of this Full Moon is for you, find your Star sign or Rising sign here, see which House is involved, and then read 'A Quick Guide to the Houses' (*see page 25*): Aries – 4th House; Taurus – 3rd House; Gemini – 2nd House; Cancer – 1st House; Leo – 12th House; Virgo – 11th House; Libra – 10th House; Scorpio – 9th House; Sagittarius – 8th House; Capricorn – 7th House; Aquarius – 6th House; Pisces – 5th House.

FULL MOON FORGIVENESS
AND QUESTIONS TO ASK

Look at where you have insecurities or fears which you need to release.
Release family dramas and upsets, including from your childhood, too.
Invite Goddess energy into your life. List what you're forgiving and
releasing, then burn the list. Join me for a free Full Moon ceremony on
Facebook (see www.moonmessages.com/fbevents).

I forgive/release:

_____

_____

_____

Who do I need to forgive from my past so that I feel whole?
(Bearing in mind that forgiving doesn't mean what happened
was okay, but rather that I've decided to let this go and move on.)

Jason, Lisa
_____

Forgiving someone else benefits me at least as much as it benefits
the person I'm forgiving? Why?

_____

What would my life look like if I could forgive everyone and
everything?

_____

This Week

Mercury goes retrograde (until 18 January 2023) and backs up into Venus, making it a great time to say those caring words of love you should have said earlier.

30 December: First Quarter Moon

☽ What Are You Grateful For This Week? ☾

_____

_____

_____

_____

_____

_____

_____

December 2022 – Week 52

26 Monday

≈ ◐

27 Tuesday

≈ ♓ ◐

28 Wednesday

♓ ◐

29 Thursday

♓ ♈ ◐

30 Friday

First Quarter Moon ♈ ◐

31 Saturday

♈ ♉ ◐

1 Sunday

♉ ◐

This Week

This week brings the first lunation of 2023: a Full Moon in the sign of Cancer. Prepare to do your first round of forgiveness work. Forgiveness transforms and transmutes energies and is something we come back to every month.

4 January: Venus moves into Aquarius

6/7 January: Full Moon occurs at 16°Cn21'

❯ Affirmation of the Week ❮

'It's only a thought,
and a thought can be changed.'

LOUISE HAY

January – Week 1

2 Monday

3 Tuesday

4 Wednesday

5 Thursday

6 Friday

Full Moon: London: 23:07 | LA: 15:07 | New York: 18:07

7 Saturday

Full Moon: Sydney: 10:07

8 Sunday

This Week

There could be some surprises to do with love or money this week. Hopefully lovely surprises... but whatever happens, do your best to b-r-e-a-t-h-e and go with the flow!

12 January: Mars retrograde ends

14 January: Third Quarter Moon

❭ What Are You Grateful For This Week? ❬

_____

_____

_____

_____

_____

_____

January – Week 2

9 Monday

♌︎○

___

10 Tuesday

♌︎♍︎○

___

11 Wednesday

♍︎○

___

12 Thursday

♍︎○

___

13 Friday

♍︎♎︎◐

___

14 Saturday

Third Quarter Moon

♎︎◑

___

15 Sunday

♎︎♏︎♐︎◑

___

Super New Moon in Aquarius

KEY WORDS AND IDEAS FOR THIS LUNATION:

- Be devoted
- Release fears
- Make a deal
- Be detached

DATE AND TIME OF THIS MOON

London: 21 Jan, 20:53 | Sydney: 22 Jan, 07:53 | LA: 21 Jan, 12:53 | New York: 21 Jan, 15:53

This is a potentially very powerful New Moon, plus it's a Supermoon. It's the first New Moon of 2023, so it's a great time to reaffirm your intentions for the year ahead, if you haven't already done that. It's also what you could call a lucky New Moon for everyone. This is because it's making a harmonious aspect to the planet of good luck and good times, Jupiter.

Here's the thing: in astrology, the impact of any New Moon depends a lot on what aspects that New Moon is making to other planets at the time.

> **This New Moon will be communing with the lucky planet Jupiter, so it really should be a positive period for us all, if potentially excessive.**

Have a good look at where the New Moon is affecting you in the 'How to Work with This Moon' section on the following page. It's where you're getting a restart – with a bit of luck on your side.

The only thing to note is that, at the same time as the New Moon, Venus is meeting Saturn. Venus is the planet of love and Saturn is the planet of longevity and lessons. If you're feeling sad, lonely or blue, seek out friends you love – the Aquarian energy is great for groups and networks. It's also a good time to cut a deal or make a long-term commitment to someone... but not a great time to be alone unless you really feel like it! Seek out new friendships if old ones feel outdated.

One thing you could include on your New Moon wish list: to make New Moon wishes every month this year!

Commit to a Restart

As you'll see, at every New Moon I'll be encouraging you to make wishes and commitments to yourself, and to send your intentions out into the Universe. Your challenge this month is to just do it. Get started. Whatever else you do, make sure you fill out the upcoming wishes and intentions questions for this month, so you get in to good habits as the year begins!

How to Work with This Moon

To discover where the energy of this New Moon is for you, find your Star sign or Rising sign here, see which House is involved, and then read 'A Quick Guide to the Houses' (see page 25): Aries – 11th House; Taurus – 10th House; Gemini – 9th House; Cancer – 8th House; Leo – 7th House; Virgo – 6th House; Libra – 5th House; Scorpio – 4th House; Sagittarius – 3rd House; Capricorn – 2nd House; Aquarius – 1st House; Pisces – 12th House.

NEW MOON WISHES AND INTENTIONS

My current biggest, most audacious goal, wish or intention is:

to do a real push up

Now turn it into an affirmation. Write it here as if it's already happened and keep repeating it until the Full Moon.

I'm strong enough to do a real
push up.

Action steps I'm going to take towards this goal:

In the next 24 hours

3 sets 10 rep counter push up

In the coming week

3 sets 10 rep, 60s plank, 5 attempts real

In the month ahead

3 st 5 rep chain push up

Tip: Write these actions you can take in the diary.

I commit to this goal whole-heartedly!

Sign here:

Vanessa Lau

This Week

Mercury ends his retrograde cycle on 18 January. The end of a Mercury retrograde cycle can be the most confusing, so go easy!

18 January: Mercury retrograde ends

20 January: the Sun moves into Aquarius

21/22 January: Super New Moon occurs at 01°Aq32'

22 January: Uranus retrograde ends

Affirmation of the Week

'Life loves me!'

LOUISE HAY

January – Week 3

16 Monday

♏ ⚊ ◑

17 Tuesday

♏ ⚊ ♐ ◑

18 Wednesday

♐ ◑

19 Thursday

♐ ⚊ ♑ ◑

20 Friday

♑ ●

21 Saturday

Super New Moon: London: 20:53 | LA: 12:53 | New York: 15:53   ♑ ♒ ●

22 Sunday

Super New Moon: Sydney: 07:53   ♒ ●

This Week

Speak particularly kindly around 26 January.
There is a Mercury (communications) clash with Chiron
(wounds and healing), which could be intense!

27 January: Venus moves into Pisces

28 January: First Quarter Moon

❯ What Are You Grateful For This Week? ❮

_____

_____

_____

_____

_____

_____

January – Week 4

23 Monday

♒︎ ♓︎ ●

---

24 Tuesday

♓︎ ●

---

25 Wednesday

♓︎ ♈︎ ●

---

26 Thursday

♈︎ ◗

---

27 Friday

♈︎ ♉︎ ◗

---

28 Saturday

First Quarter Moon

♉︎ ◗

29 Sunday

♉︎ ◗

February

February brings Valentine's Day, so it's always a good time to do a kind of romantic check-in. How are you doing in all your most important relationships, romantic or otherwise? As the month begins, Venus, the planet of love, is in arguably the most romantic sign, Pisces. So that's already a pretty good set-up. Moreover, on Valentine's night, pretty much wherever you are in the world, there is a luscious link between loving Venus and numinous Neptune.

On the one hand, this is a potentially dissolve-in-love alignment. On the other, though, if you're with someone you know you can't trust or you're chasing someone you secretly suspect isn't available, there could be a let-down mid-month. So keep your eyes wide open!

Overall, the month looks positive. If you want to make the most of the energies, be willing to make changes when it comes to your most important relationships. Also stay open to changes to do with money, be responsible and do what you said you were going to do.

It's also a good month for communications, so whether you have love on your mind or something else altogether, do keep talking. The peak dates for communications are 6, 10, 17–18, 20 and 22 February. In particular, if you have to have an important conversation with someone, 17 or 18 February is ideal for that.

Another main theme this month is healing, so ask yourself where you need healing and work on it throughout February. Maybe you need to release something, forgive yourself or someone else, or just gather your strength.

This month I will:
- ❑ Re-find the romance
- ❑ Aim for healing
- ❑ Be a grown-up

Full Moon
in Leo

KEY WORDS AND IDEAS
FOR THIS LUNATION:

- Focus on healing energies
- Dream
- Meditate
- Seek inspiration

DATE AND TIME OF THIS MOON
London: 5 Feb, 18:28 | Sydney: 6 Feb, 05:28 | LA: 5 Feb, 10:28 | New York: 5 Feb, 13:28

There could be some shocks or surprises leading up to the Full Moon, so go easy as we approach it. Remember, when the Full Moon takes place, all our emotions swell, just like the Full Moon. Just before the Full Moon occurs, the Sun and Moon will clash with the planet of chaos, Uranus. If you're already feeling anxious or nervous about something, you must remember to really work on yourself in the lead-up to the Full Moon, using breathing, meditation or whatever else you find helpful.

This month the Full Moon is taking place in the sign of Leo, which is of course the sign of pride. The Full Moon in Leo takes place when the Sun is in Aquarius and the Moon is in Leo, on the exact opposite side of the zodiac.

> This month, think about whether you've been allowing your ego to get in your way. Or maybe you actually need to be a little bit prouder of yourself? Any conflict should be resolved based upon which approach is more practical – even if it's an oddball solution.

Aquarius is a very detached sign and able to be aloof and cool; Leo is a fire sign and can get very wound up in ego. Remember, we all have all 12 signs in our chart – this is not a commentary on Leo or Aquarius people!

If You Couldn't Fail...

The worst thing about our ego is that it often makes us behave in a way that we otherwise wouldn't. Sometimes that can actually hinder our progress. So this month, take a moment to work with the energy of the Full Moon by grabbing a sheet of paper and a pen. Write at the top 'What I Would Do If I Knew I Couldn't Fail', and then describe this on the rest of the page. This exercise will help you get an idea of where ego (or fear) may be holding you back. Do the exercise on the night of the Full Moon, if you possibly can.

How to Work with This Moon

To discover where the energy of this Full Moon is for you, find your Star sign or Rising sign here, see which House is involved, and then read 'A Quick Guide to the Houses' (see page 25): Aries – 5th House; Taurus – 4th House; Gemini – 3rd House; Cancer – 2nd House; Leo – 1st House; Virgo – 12th House; Libra – 11th House; Scorpio – 10th House; Sagittarius – 9th House; Capricorn – 8th House; Aquarius – 7th House; Pisces – 6th House.

FULL MOON FORGIVENESS
AND QUESTIONS TO ASK

This Valentine's month, think about whether you need to forgive any of your past romantic partners. Or maybe you need to forgive yourself for the way you behaved in a past relationship? Also, with regards to relationships, what are you resisting? Join me for a free Full Moon ritual via www.moonmessages.com/fbevents.

I forgive/release:

nothing to forgive exs they taught me what
want don't want + help me understand my
clients they fulfilled their soul contract
- forgive Lisa not good fit don't trust her

Thinking about my biggest issue, what would I love to do?

buy my dream home. easily lose weight
build strength be consistent

What could I do to get more inspired this month?

move lighten up journal

What could I do to better balance my own needs with the needs of my friends?

actually have friends stop isolating

This Week

It's a Full Moon week, so get ready for emotions to be running a little higher than usual. Make 'No rash reactions' your motto for the week. Also, this is an awesome week for spiritual practices such as meditation, poetry-writing and journalling.

1 February: festivals of Imbolc (northern hemisphere) and Lammas (southern hemisphere)

5/6 February: Full Moon occurs at 16°Le40'

❯ Affirmation of the Week ❮

'I am comfortable looking in the mirror, saying, "I love you, I really love you."'

Louise Hay

January/February – Week 5

30 Monday

31 Tuesday

1 Wednesday

2 Thursday

3 Friday

4 Saturday

5 Sunday

Full Moon: LA: 10:28 | New York: 13:28 | London: 18:28

This Week

This could be an absolutely lovely week for romance. If you know you're with the right person, you could feel as though you have your head in the clouds. If you're involved with someone you know is untrustworthy, ask yourself 'why?!'

11 February: Mercury moves into Aquarius

❱ What Are You Grateful For This Week? ❰

_____

_____

_____

_____

_____

_____

February – Week 6

6 Monday

Full Moon: Sydney: 05:28 _____ ♌ ♍ ○

7 Tuesday

_____ ♍ ○

8 Wednesday

_____ ♍ ○

9 Thursday

_____ ♍ ♎ ◐

10 Friday

_____ ♎ ◐

11 Saturday

_____ ♎ ♏ ◐

12 Sunday

_____ ♏ ◐

This Week

The ideal date on which to have a tricky conversation, make a big presentation, or do anything else that requires very good communication skills, is 17 February. Also, there is a lot of love and passion in the air this week.

13 February: Third Quarter Moon

18 February: the Sun moves into Pisces

19/20 February: Super New Moon occurs at 01°Pi22'

☽ What Are You Grateful For This Week? ☾

_____

_____

_____

_____

_____

February – Week 7

13 Monday

Third Quarter Moon

14 Tuesday

15 Wednesday

16 Thursday

17 Friday

18 Saturday

19 Sunday

Super New Moon: LA: 23:05

Super New Moon in Pisces

KEY WORDS AND IDEAS FOR THIS LUNATION:

- Mystical moments
- Healing opportunities
- Change your mind
- Destiny calling

If you're on the spiritual path, and chances are that if you're reading this diary, you probably are, then this is a really important New Moon to pay attention to. It's in the very mystical sign of Pisces, and it's a very gentle and inspiring lunation.

Pisces is the last sign of the zodiac and is where we dream. What are your dreams for yourself and the people you love in the year ahead? Now is the time to imagine them as reality. Feel them as real in your body as you do the New Moon exercises on the following pages. Feeling them as real is the first step to manifesting them.

Also note that this New Moon is making what's called an 'out-of-sign conjunction' to Saturn, the planet of hard work, responsibilities, challenges and commitments. The conjunction is when the planets are in the same place at the same time within a few degrees of each other (each sign has 30 degrees). In this case, Saturn is in the last degrees of Aquarius and the New Moon is taking place just a few degrees away in early Pisces.

So if there's something you need to do in your life to make your dreams more concrete, now is the time to commit to that. Saturn has a fearsome reputation but is actually the planet that helps us concretize our intentions.

Meditate, Meditate, Meditate

Among other things, Pisces is the sign of meditation. Meditation will change your life by helping you to connect to the unified field of all there is. Once you do that, your life will start to change in ways you probably never imagined possible.

So this month, if you're not already regularly meditating, set yourself the task of meditating every single day for 15–20 minutes (I use the Insight Timer app to keep track of time). Just sit quietly and breathe. Play some gentle music if you like. If it helps, you can chant something simple like 'Om Shanti', which is an invocation of peace.

How to Work with This Moon

To discover where the energy of this New Moon is for you, find your Star sign or Rising sign here, see which House is involved, and then read 'A Quick Guide to the Houses' (see page 25): Aries – 12th House; Taurus – 11th House; Gemini – 10th House; Cancer – 9th House; Leo – 8th House; Virgo – 7th House; Libra – 6th House; Scorpio – 5th House; Sagittarius – 4th House; Capricorn – 3rd House; Aquarius – 2nd House; Pisces – 1st House.

NEW MOON WISHES AND INTENTIONS

My current biggest, most audacious goal, wish or intention is:

_____

_____

Now turn it into an affirmation. Write it here as if it's already happened and keep repeating it until the Full Moon.

_____

_____

Action steps I'm going to take towards this goal:

In the next 24 hours

_____

In the coming week

_____

In the month ahead

_____

Tip: Write these actions you can take in the diary.

I commit to this goal whole-heartedly!

Sign here:

_____

This Week

Once the New Moon has happened, we move into the waxing cycle. That's the time to start to really pursue your goals. Be clear on what you need to do and don't let any minor hitches put you off!

19/20 February: Super New Moon occurs at 01°Pi22'

20 February: Venus moves into Aries

) Affirmation of the Week (

'All is well in my world.
Everything is working out for my highest good.
Out of this situation only good will come.
I am safe!'

Louise Hay

February – Week 8

20 Monday

Super New Moon: London: 07:05 | Sydney: 18:05 | New York: 02:05

21 Tuesday

22 Wednesday

23 Thursday

24 Friday

25 Saturday

26 Sunday

March

Full Moon: 7 March
Third Quarter Moon: 15 March
New Moon: 21/22 March
First Quarter Moon: 29 March

If you're looking for a big month to do big things, this is definitely it! March sees two major alignments. Each of these would be worth doing entire workshops on, but let's boil them down here.

On 7 March, we get the movement of Saturn – the serious planet of commitment and longevity, hard work and hard lessons – changing signs. Saturn will be moving into the last sign of the zodiac, Pisces. For each of us this will mean something different, but know this: wherever Saturn goes, lessons follow. To find out where in your chart Pisces is (and therefore how this will affect you), see the Super New Moon in Pisces lunation (*page 76*). The House that's being activated by the New Moon in Pisces is the same House that's being triggered by Saturn now. Expect lessons in that part of your life.

Then on 23 March, we have transformative Pluto – the planet that explodes everything, is the volcano of the zodiac and is all about passion, power and getting rid of what's no longer working or even toxic – changing signs and moving into Aquarius. This is a temporary move, as Pluto will be retrograding between Capricorn and Aquarius from now until 2024. To work out where you're getting this blast in your chart, see the Super New Moon in Aquarius (*page 56*). The same House being triggered by the New Moon is where you're getting this massive blast of power to clear away dead wood.

Because March is so massive astrologically, it's a month to live really intentionally and consciously. Focus on your spiritual practices and listen to your inner-tuition more than ever.

This month I will:
- ❏ Blast away the past
- ❏ Get disciplined in my spiritual practice
- ❏ Focus on healing

This Week

We're moving towards the end of the current cycle of Saturn in Aquarius. It started back in March 2020 and wrought a lot of hard lessons on humanity. It ends next week. So this week, contemplate: what have we learned?

27 February: First Quarter Moon

2 March: Mercury moves into Pisces

❨ What Are You Grateful For This Week? ❩

_____

_____

_____

_____

_____

_____

February/March – Week 9

27 Monday

First Quarter Moon

28 Tuesday

1 Wednesday

2 Thursday

3 Friday

4 Saturday

5 Sunday

Full Moon
in Virgo

KEY WORDS AND IDEAS
FOR THIS LUNATION:

- End of an era
- Balance spirituality and practicality
- Be of service
- Be kind

DATE AND TIME OF THIS MOON

London: 7 Mar, 12:40 | Sydney: 7 Mar, 23:40 | LA: 7 Mar, 04:40 | New York: 7 Mar, 07:40

Expect this to be an extremely powerful Full Moon. It's taking place just as the planet of hard work and hard facts, Saturn, finally changes signs and moves from Aquarius into Pisces. Saturn is not to be feared because it's powerful; Saturn makes us stronger and more resilient. However, its sojourn once every 30 years through the sign of Aquarius coincided with the pandemic years we've all just lived through. That cycle officially ends now, and hopefully the last vestiges of the pandemic do too.

The Full Moon is in the sign of Virgo, as mentioned, and that's the sign associated with alternative health. Think about what lessons you've learned about your health, and about alternative health treatments, in the past few years. Think about how you could look after yourself better now and into the future.

> There could be some confusion in the air this week as the Full Moon takes place. Mars and Neptune are clashing, so you may find that you're not exactly sure where to put your energy.

If that's how you're feeling, here are a few ideas to help, based on the overall energies: make space in your home by decluttering; consider volunteer work of some kind (it's a great way to meet people with similar values while helping others); sort out an upset with a friend; make a plan to eat more healthily – and stick to it; write up ideas for morning and evening routines; balance your finances; meditate daily; and clean out your fridge.

Make a Spiritual Plan

It may feel counterintuitive to make a plan at Full Moon, since usually we begin things at New Moon. But all the energies this month really do add up to one thing: it's the ideal time to decide what in your life you need to release to make space for your spiritual pursuits. So make a plan for what you'd like to do spiritually in the coming two years. That's approximately how long plan-loving Saturn will be in the spiritual sign of Pisces. The energy of the Virgo Full Moon is also perfect for careful, long-range planning.

How to Work with This Moon

To discover where the energy of this Full Moon is for you, find your Star sign or Rising sign here, see which House is involved, and then read 'A Quick Guide to the Houses' (see page 25): Aries – 6th House; Taurus – 5th House; Gemini – 4th House; Cancer – 3rd House; Leo – 2nd House; Virgo – 1st House; Libra – 12th House; Scorpio – 11th House; Sagittarius – 10th House; Capricorn – 9th House; Aquarius – 8th House; Pisces – 7th House.

FULL MOON FORGIVENESS AND QUESTIONS TO ASK

It's tempting to say that if you only do one Full Moon Forgiveness and Questions to Ask ritual this year, make it this one! The overall combined energies right now really are supercharged. It's the ideal time to release the past, and often forgiving is the best way to do that. Also, what are you releasing resistance to? Join me for a free Full Moon ritual via www.moonmessages.com/fbevents.

I forgive/release:

_____

_____

_____

_____

What am I holding on to from the past that's weighing me down?

_____

What is my priority for my spiritual life in the coming two years?

_____

Where in my life do I need to be more organized and how would it help?

_____

This Week

This week, the planet of good luck, Jupiter, meets the planetoid of healing, Chiron. Tap into this if you need it by dedicating the week to your healing – spiritually, emotionally or physically.

7 March: Full Moon occurs at 16°Vi40';
Saturn moves into Pisces

☽ Affirmation of the Week ☾

'It is safe to look within.'

LOUISE HAY

March – Week 10

6 Monday

♌︎♍︎○

7 Tuesday

Full Moon: London: 12:40 | Sydney: 23:40 | LA: 04:40 | New York: 07:40

♍︎○

8 Wednesday

♍︎♎︎○

9 Thursday

♎︎○

10 Friday

♎︎○

11 Saturday

♎︎♏︎○

12 Sunday

♏︎○

This Week

As the week begins, we're still riding the beautiful waves of a Jupiter–Chiron meeting. Jupiter is the planet of optimism and plenty, while Chiron is the healing planetoid. What do you need to heal? Envisage it healed.

15 March: Third Quarter Moon

16 March: Venus moves into Taurus

19 March: Mercury moves into Aries

☽ What Are You Grateful For This Week? ☾

March – Week 11

13 Monday

♏ ♐ ◐

14 Tuesday

♐ ◐

15 Wednesday

Third Quarter Moon

♐ ♑ ◐

16 Thursday

♑ ◐

17 Friday

♑ ♒ ◐

18 Saturday

♒ ◐

19 Sunday

♒ ♓ ◐

New Moon in Aries

KEY WORDS AND IDEAS FOR THIS LUNATION:

- Heal your thoughts
- Heal your life
- Be optimistic
- Start afresh

DATE AND TIME OF THIS MOON

London: 21 Mar, 17:23 | Sydney: 22 Mar, 04:23 | LA: 21 Mar, 10:23 | New York: 21 Mar, 13:23

The first thing to say is that if you're just starting to work with the diary now, don't panic! Yes, you've missed the first couple of months, but you're tuning in at a very good time. This month brings the New Moon in the first sign of the zodiac, Aries. In other words, it's a really perfect time to start all over again.

> Aries is the first sign of the zodiac, which means we're now at the start of a new full lunar cycle that will see New Moons happening in all 12 signs of the zodiac over the coming year.

This New Moon takes place against the background of one of the biggest events of the astrological year: the move of the power planet Pluto from Capricorn into Aquarius. This new placement lasts until early June when Pluto retrogrades back into Capricorn.

For thousands of years, people (mainly women, but also some enlightened men) made magic by the light and the dark of the Moon. Then everything changed, and women who practised Moon magic were put to death by flames. As you can imagine, as a result such magical practices either went underground or, in many cases, stopped altogether. Women no longer told their daughters the secrets of the Moon. Until now. The Divine Feminine is re-emerging, and with it magical practices such as intention-setting at New Moon and resistance-release at... Full Moon. So are you in? If so, sign the pledge on the next page to connect with each New and Full Moon in the year ahead.

Pledge to Connect

I, ————————————————————————— , do hereby pledge myself to connect with the New and Full Moons each month, to expand my conscious awareness and my connection to the cosmic and the Divine.

Signed ——————————————————————

Date ——————————————————————

How to Work with This Moon

To discover where the energy of this New Moon is for you, find your Star sign or Rising sign here, see which House is involved, and then read 'A Quick Guide to the Houses' (see page 25): Aries – 1st House; Taurus – 12th House; Gemini – 11th House; Cancer – 10th House; Leo – 9th House; Virgo – 8th House; Libra – 7th House; Scorpio – 6th House; Sagittarius – 5th House; Capricorn – 4th House; Aquarius – 3rd House; Pisces – 2nd House.

NEW MOON WISHES AND INTENTIONS

My current biggest, most audacious goal, wish or intention is:

_____

_____

Now turn it into an affirmation. Write it here as if it's already happened and keep repeating it until the Full Moon.

_____

_____

Action steps I'm going to take towards this goal:

In the next 24 hours

_____

In the coming week

_____

In the month ahead

_____

Tip: Write these actions you can take in the diary.

I commit to this goal whole-heartedly!

Sign here:

_____

This Week

This week sees the mighty Pluto changing signs and moving into Aquarius, which can show up outdated ways of thinking.

20 March: Spring Equinox/Ostara (northern hemisphere) and Autumn Equinox/Mabon (southern hemisphere)

20 March: the Sun moves into Aries, marking the first Cardinal ingress of the year. Check into the Diary Bonuses area (www.moonmessages.com/diarybonuses2023) for your 'Reflect and Review' worksheet

21/22 March: New Moon occurs at 00°Ar49'

23 March: Pluto moves into Aquarius

25 March: Mars moves into Cancer

❯ Affirmation of the Week ❮

'The point of power is always in the present moment.'

LOUISE HAY

March – Week 12

20 Monday

♓ ◖

21 Tuesday

New Moon: London: 17:23 | LA: 10:23 | New York: 13:23

♓ ♈ ◯

22 Wednesday

New Moon: Sydney: 04:23

♈ ◯

23 Thursday

♈ ♉ ◗

24 Friday

♉ ◗

25 Saturday

♉ ◗

26 Sunday

♉ ♊ ◗

This Week

It's a week when good things can happen quickly, especially those to do with love and money. Be confident that whatever efforts you make this week are going to pay off. Think positively and this week could be wonderful.

29 March: First Quarter Moon

❱ What Are You Grateful For This Week? ❰

_____

_____

_____

_____

_____

_____

_____

March/April – Week 13

27 Monday

28 Tuesday

29 Wednesday

First Quarter Moon

30 Thursday

31 Friday

1 Saturday

2 Sunday

April

Full Moon: 5/6 April
Third Quarter Moon: 13 April
New Moon: 19/20 April
First Quarter Moon: 27 April

The astrological energetic pace is picking up right now. Last month we had the moves of mighty Saturn and Pluto into new signs, bringing with them a whole new gust of energy. And this month, we move into the first eclipse season of the year.

Eclipses are times of high energies and they often open up portals to change. They used to be feared in the old days, but these days, most astrologers will tell you that, used correctly, eclipses can help you release the past and step into the future you know you were born for.

The good news is that this month's eclipse is a New Moon eclipse, which is especially great because it'll more or less supercharge any intentions that you send out to the Universe.

This eclipse is taking place in the last degree of Aries and is the second New Moon in Aries in a row. As you might remember, the New Moon was in the same sign last month. In other words, wherever in your chart this New Moon eclipse is activating, you're getting a second chance to use it (or lose it)!

Note that the New Moon is also communing with Pluto, newly arrived in Aquarius, which means: whatever is inauthentic has to go; if you're troubled, seek a win-win outcome; act for the good of all or not at all; and detox, detox, detox your mind, body and spirit!

Be aware that this eclipse could bring up a lot of stuff (that's a polite way of putting it!). Even if you feel as though the ground is quaking this month, know that it's for the best eventually, on some level.

This month I will:
❑ **Change my life in some way**
❑ **Leave the past behind**
❑ **Be bold**

Full Moon
in Libra

KEY WORDS AND IDEAS
FOR THIS LUNATION:

- Tensions in the air
- Romantic developments
- Someone is being stubborn
- Compromise is needed

This is a very powerful Full Moon. For a start, it's taking place in the relationship-oriented sign of Libra. So while the Sun is in fiery Aries, the Moon is in Libra, the sign that wants harmony. Aries is all me, me, me and Libra is all you, you, you.

At the time of this Full Moon, there may be a clash between what you want versus what someone else wants. The good news is that Libra is the sign that likes things to be nice, so hopefully you can move towards that, if times have been tough.

One thing that distinguishes this Libra Full Moon in 2023 is the fact that there are two rather big astrological alignments taking place at around the same time.

One is what's called a T-Square and the other a Grand Trine. Put them together and there is a definite feeling of pressure being piled on someone (it could be on you, or maybe you're doing the piling on!). But there is also release available – you just have to find out how to let it all go.

The challenge is that there are very fixed energies around, so you're going to have to be extremely determined to release. Try the following exercise to help, then use the space on page 105 to write down what you're releasing resistance to.

Tap Away Resistance

Tapping, also known as EFT (Emotional Freedom Techniques), is a powerful way to release unresolved issues, relieve stress and restore balance to your life. With your fingers, you tap on specific meridian points of the body, which sends a calming signal to the brain. By restoring this energy balance you can relieve stress and anxiety, and release emotions and any resistance you may have. Any Full Moon is a great time to release resistance, but this one is possibly one of the greatest of them all for 2023! So, if you've been resisting but are now 100 per cent ready to release, then visit www.moonmessages. com/resisting for a powerful video about tapping and how it can help you.

How to Work with This Moon

To discover where the energy of this Full Moon is for you, find your Star sign or Rising sign here, see which House is involved, and then read 'A Quick Guide to the Houses' (see page 25): Aries – 7th House; Taurus – 6th House; Gemini – 5th House; Cancer – 4th House; Leo – 3rd House; Virgo – 2nd House; Libra – 1st House; Scorpio – 12th House; Sagittarius – 11th House; Capricorn – 10th House; Aquarius – 9th House; Pisces – 8th House.

FULL MOON FORGIVENESS
AND QUESTIONS TO ASK

Any month is a good month to release relationship dramas, but this month's Full Moon is especially good for that. This is because it's in the relationship sign of Libra. So can you include on your list forgiving someone who hurt you (or even someone you love)? You can forgive but not forget — so you lose the pain but not the lesson. The Full Moon in Libra really is one of the best times of the year to move on from a past relationship hurt, whether it's with someone who's still in your life or someone you haven't seen in years but still need to forgive. Letting go like that will actually free you up. Join me for a free Full Moon ritual via www.moonmessages.com/fbevents.

I forgive/release:

_____

_____

What are you resisting — what do you really want that isn't happening yet?

_____

Where do you think this resistance comes from?

_____

What would your life look like if you were willing to release this resistance?

_____

This Week

The Full Moon in Libra this week is a time to take the path of least resistance. Luck and healing are in the air, too, which should make life easier.

3 April: Mercury moves into Taurus

5/6 April: Full Moon occurs at 16°Li07′

❨ Affirmation of the Week ❩

'I forgive myself
and set myself free.'

LOUISE HAY

April – Week 14

3 Monday

♍ ○

4 Tuesday

♍ ♎ ○

5 Wednesday

Full Moon: LA: 21:34

♎ ○

6 Thursday

Full Moon: London: 05:34 | Sydney: 14:34 | New York: 00:34

♎ ○

7 Friday

♎ ♏ ○

8 Saturday

♏ ○

9 Sunday

♏ ♐ ○

This Week

Focus on positivity this week — there should be a lot of it about.

11 April: Venus moves into Gemini

13 April: Third Quarter Moon

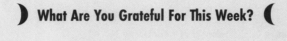

☽ What Are You Grateful For This Week? ☾

_____

_____

_____

_____

_____

_____

_____

April – Week 15

10 Monday

♐ ◗

11 Tuesday

♐ ♑ ◗

12 Wednesday

♑ ◗

13 Thursday

Third Quarter Moon

♑ ♒ ◑

14 Friday

♒ ◑

15 Saturday

♒ ♓ ◑

16 Sunday

♓ ◑

New Moon
Eclipse in Aries

KEY WORDS AND IDEAS
FOR THIS LUNATION:

- Excitement
- Second chances
- Brave moves
- Restarts

This is big. Not only is it a New Moon, but it's a New Moon eclipse, plus it's the second New Moon in the sign of Aries in a row... and it's clashing with Pluto. Let's break all that down.

As you hopefully know by now, every New Moon brings an amazing chance to start all over again in one part of your life. Which part of your life that is depends on where in your chart it's activating – that's what the 'How to Work with This Moon' section on the following page is about. A New Moon eclipse, however, is all that and more.

A New Moon eclipse is way more powerful than a regular New Moon. This one is making what's called an out-of-sign alignment with the planet of detox and transformation, Pluto. So it's urging us to release the past to make room for what we want in our present and our future, and is a great opportunity to make change from the inside out. It's a super important lunation so make sure you join me on Facebook (visit www.moonmessages.com/fbevents) for a New Moon ritual.

> **This New Moon has themes of releasing, letting go and flushing away anything that no longer serves your highest good.**

The fact that it's the second Aries New Moon in a row means that you've had two New Moons in a row in the same part of your chart – you could see this second New Moon in Aries as a second chance. Read on for info about how to work out where it's hitting you.

A Second Chance...

Take a moment to look at the 'How to Work with This Moon' section below. Work out where in your chart the New Moon eclipse is taking place. Bearing in mind that eclipses are an opportunity to get off the wrong path and onto the right one, what does this mean for you? Grab your journal and make some notes about how you plan to use this second chance for a restart in this part of your life. Just write freely for a good 10 minutes. If you don't like to write, you could record your thoughts on your phone.

How to Work with This Moon

To discover where the energy of this New Moon is for you, find your Star sign or Rising sign here, see which House is involved, and then read 'A Quick Guide to the Houses' (see page 25): Aries – 1st House; Taurus – 12th House; Gemini – 11th House; Cancer – 10th House; Leo – 9th House; Virgo – 8th House; Libra – 7th House; Scorpio – 6th House; Sagittarius – 5th House; Capricorn – 4th House; Aquarius – 3rd House; Pisces – 2nd House.

NEW MOON WISHES AND INTENTIONS

My current biggest, most audacious goal, wish or intention is:

_____

_____

Now turn it into an affirmation. Write it here as if it's already happened and keep repeating it until the Full Moon.

_____

_____

Action steps I'm going to take towards this goal:

In the next 24 hours

_____

In the coming week

_____

In the month ahead

_____

Tip: Write these actions you can take in the diary.

I commit to this goal whole-heartedly!

Sign here:

_____

This Week

Mercury goes retrograde on 21 April, this time in the sign of Taurus. When it comes to the flow of abundance in your life, where could you use a do-over?

19/20 April: New Moon eclipse occurs at 29°Ar50′

20 April: the Sun moves into Taurus

21 April: Mercury goes retrograde (until 14 May)

☽ Affirmation of the Week ☾

'I am in the process
of positive change.'

LOUISE HAY

April – Week 16

17 Monday

♓ ●

18 Tuesday

♓ ♈ ●

19 Wednesday

New Moon eclipse: LA: 21:12

♈ ●

20 Thursday

New Moon eclipse: London: 05:12 | Sydney: 14:12 | New York: 00:12

♈ ♉ ●

21 Friday

♉ ●

22 Saturday

♉ ♊ ◐

23 Sunday

♊ ●

This Week

Overall this is a pretty positive week and good things can happen quickly, thanks to some harmonious planetary alignments and the Waxing Moon in eclipse season.

27 April: First Quarter Moon

❯ What Are You Grateful For This Week? ❮

_____

_____

_____

_____

_____

_____

April – Week 17

24 Monday

♊ ♋ 🌓

25 Tuesday

♋ 🌓

26 Wednesday

♋ 🌓

27 Thursday

First Quarter Moon

♋ ♌ 🌓

28 Friday

♌ 🌓

29 Saturday

♌ ♍ 🌓

30 Sunday

♍ 🌓

May

Full Moon: 5/6 May
Third Quarter Moon: 12 May
New Moon: 19/20 May
First Quarter Moon: 27 May

Astrologically speaking, May is a pretty big month. Arguably the three biggest events of the month are (in the following order): a Full Moon eclipse in the sign of Scorpio on 5 May; the end of Mercury retrograde in the sign of Taurus on 15 May; and the move of the mighty planet Jupiter into the sign of cash, Taurus, on 16 May. Jupiter was last in Taurus in 2012. This time around, it'll stay in Taurus until May next year.

Also note that the first major alignment Jupiter makes after moving into Taurus is a clash with Pluto, the planet of the pandemic. I write this a year or so before you read it, so at the time of writing we're all hoping that by 2023, the pandemic will be just a memory. However, there could be a reminder of it this month. Fingers crossed there isn't!

Other than that, Jupiter is actually going to be making some positive alignment as he moves through Taurus, which means life should be a little easier for us all.

If you want to see which House Jupiter will be in for you now and through until 2024, have a look at the 'How to Work with This Moon' section for the Black New Moon in Taurus (see page 130) – whatever House you see there is the part of your life that's being touched by lucky Jupiter.

This month I will:
- ❑ Think about what I want to expand in my life
- ❑ Be grateful for where I feel lucky
- ❑ Release anything that holds me back

Full Moon Eclipse in Scorpio

KEY WORDS AND IDEAS
FOR THIS LUNATION:

- Release!
- Drop a grudge
- Allow for changes
- Speak your mind

DATE AND TIME OF THIS MOON

London: 5 May, 18:34 | Sydney: 6 May, 03:34 | LA: 5 May, 10:34 | New York: 5 May, 13:34

If ever there was a month to make detox your aim, this is it. This Full Moon is taking place in the sign of Scorpio. Hopefully I've driven the message home enough now about how we all have all 12 signs in our chart. So even if you're not a Scorpio, you have the sign of Scorpio in your chart somewhere. That's just how it works.

Note that wherever you have Scorpio, that's where things for you are deeper and more meaningful, but also where you may have more black moods and find it harder to release grudges.

> This Full Moon eclipse is taking place just as Jupiter is preparing to smash up against detox planet Pluto. In other words, if we add the release aspect of the Full Moon eclipse to the Jupiter–Pluto energies, we have the perfect storm needed to help us release the past and let go.

If you believe you may have been somehow traumatized by the pandemic years, this is a really good time to do some kind of ceremony. You may want to focus on the fact that you're still here and to be grateful for that. Energetically speaking, it really is a super-powerful time at the moment. Do ensure that you make time to meditate, to consult your Oracle cards, to journal and hopefully to join with me in a free Full Moon ritual (www.moonmessages.com/fbevents), or do one of your own.

Let it Go, Let it Go!

The Full Moon eclipse in Scorpio coupled with the upcoming Jupiter–Pluto clash late this month means that now is the perfect time to do release work. As well as filling out the pages overleaf, it's the perfect time for a very powerful chant to the Goddess Kali, the destroyer goddess, who helps us release anything negative, especially fear. Decide what you need to release and then chant 'Om Kali-yei Namaha' for at least 10 minutes. If you haven't accessed the diary area (www.moonmessages.com/diarybonuses2023) yet, do so now and you'll find this chant there as well.

How to Work with This Moon

To discover where the energy of this Full Moon is for you, find your Star sign or Rising sign here, see which House is involved, and then read 'A Quick Guide to the Houses' (*see page 25*): Aries – 8th House; Taurus – 7th House; Gemini – 6th House; Cancer – 5th House; Leo – 4th House; Virgo – 3rd House; Libra – 2nd House; Scorpio – 1st House; Sagittarius – 12th House; Capricorn – 11th House; Aquarius – 10th House; Pisces – 9th House.

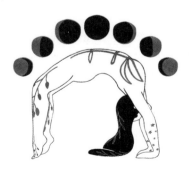

FULL MOON FORGIVENESS AND QUESTIONS TO ASK

Every month is an amazing month to do forgiveness and release work, but hand on heart, May 2023 is better than most months! Make sure you take some time to fill in this page. It's not too hard to do and it really can change your energy and therefore your life. Remember these wise words from the wonderful Louise Hay: 'Those on the spiritual pathway know the importance of forgiveness.' Join me for a free Full Moon ritual via www.moonmessages.com/fbevents.

I forgive/release:

_____

_____

_____

_____

Can I forgive the person who hurt me most and how would I feel if I did that?

_____

_____

What part of my life can I now turn the page on?

_____

_____

This Week

It's a Full Moon eclipse week so live consciously and intentionally. Sense your feelings as they come up and consciously process them. This is the first step to detoxing and letting them go.

1 May: festivals of Beltane (northern hemisphere) and Samhain (southern hemisphere); Pluto goes retrograde (until 11 October 2023)

5/6 May: Full Moon eclipse occurs at 14°Sc58'

7 May: Venus moves into Cancer

☽ Affirmation of the Week ☾

'I now go beyond other people's fears and limitations.'

LOUISE HAY

May – Week 18

1 Monday

♍ ○

2 Tuesday

♍ ♎ ○

3 Wednesday

♎ ○

4 Thursday

♎ ♏ ○

5 Friday

Full Moon eclipse: London: 18:34 | LA: 10:34 | New York: 13:34

♏ ○

6 Saturday

Full Moon eclipse: Sydney: 03:34

♏ ♐ ○

7 Sunday

♐ ○

This Week

A very good week to make a deal or declare your feelings for someone. We're in the waning cycle, which is usually about letting go — but the commitment in the force is strong!

12 May: Third Quarter Moon

☽ What Are You Grateful For This Week? ☾

_____

_____

_____

_____

_____

_____

May – Week 19

8 Monday

_____ ♐♑ ○

9 Tuesday

_____ ♑ ○

10 Wednesday

_____ ♑ ◑

11 Thursday

_____ ♑♒ ◑

12 Friday

Third Quarter Moon ♒ ◑

13 Saturday

_____ ♒♓ ◑

14 Sunday

_____ ♓ ◑

Black New Moon in Taurus

KEY WORDS AND IDEAS FOR THIS LUNATION:

- Exciting
- Friction
- Abundance-attracting
- Focused

DATE AND TIME OF THIS MOON

London: 19 May, 16:53 | Sydney: 20 May, 01:53 | LA: 19 May, 08:53 | New York: 19 May, 11:53

There is quite a lot to unpack with this New Moon. For a start, it's called a Black Moon because it's the third New Moon in a season (spring in the northern hemisphere; autumn Down Under) that has four New Moons. The good news here is that we're pretty much through the most challenging part of the year now.

Hopefully you've sailed through so far, and if so, that augurs well for the rest of 2023. Not that it's going to be 100 per cent easy, of course. It never is!

> We're on this planet to evolve, and any challenges that come our way should be viewed through that lens if at all possible. Use this New Moon to affirm that you're going to make the most of the rest of 2023.

The New Moon is making what's called an 'out-of-sign' aspect to Pluto, the planet of power and passion, and also to Mars, the planet of drive and determination. This suggests there will be a lot of energy to get things done. What's on your to-do list? It also suggests that, even if you've gone through a rough time in the last month or two, that can turn around now.

Note that Taurus is the sign of cash – it rules Wall Street (remember the Wall Street Bull?). So if you make only one wish all year about abundance, make it now! Knowing what you want is halfway to sorting the issue; then you just have to take action. It's a month when amazing things can happen. Fingers crossed!

I Affirm That...!

Choose one of these Louise Hay affirmations for abundance and pledge to recite them at least five times, twice a day, between now and the Full Moon in two weeks' time. Set a reminder alarm on your phone to do it, if you think that will help. You could also choose one to do each week.

- 'Life supplies all my needs in great abundance. I trust life.'

- 'I prosper wherever I turn.'

- 'I live in a loving, abundant, harmonious Universe, and I am grateful'

- 'I now do work I love, and I am well paid for it.'

- 'I pay my bills with love, and I rejoice as I write out each cheque. Abundance flows freely through me.'

How to Work with This Moon

To discover where the energy of this New Moon is for you, find your Star sign or Rising sign here, see which House is involved, and then read 'A Quick Guide to the Houses' (see page 25): Aries – 2nd House; Taurus – 1st House; Gemini – 12th House; Cancer – 11th House; Leo – 10th House; Virgo – 9th House; Libra – 8th House; Scorpio – 7th House; Sagittarius – 6th House; Capricorn – 5th House; Aquarius – 4th House; Pisces – 3rd House.

NEW MOON WISHES AND INTENTIONS

My current biggest, most audacious goal, wish or intention is:

_____

_____

Now turn it into an affirmation. Write it here as if it's already happened and keep repeating it until the Full Moon.

_____

_____

Action steps I'm going to take towards this goal:

In the next 24 hours

_____

In the coming week

_____

In the month ahead

_____

Tip: Write these actions you can take in the diary.

I commit to this goal whole-heartedly!

Sign here:

_____

This Week

The mighty move of lucky Jupiter into the sign of money, Taurus, happens on 16 May. Money isn't the be all and end all, but a healthy flow of it makes life easier, so make this cycle work for you!

15 May: Mercury retrograde ends

16 May: Jupiter moves into Taurus

19/20 May: Black New Moon occurs at 28°Ta25'

20 May: Mars moves into Leo

21 May: the Sun moves into Gemini

☽ Affirmation of the Week ☾

'Every thought we think is creating our future.'

LOUISE HAY

May – Week 20

15 Monday

♓♌◐

16 Tuesday

♌◐

17 Wednesday

♌♉◐

18 Thursday

♉◐

19 Friday

Black New Moon: London: 16:53 | LA: 08:53 | New York: 11:53

♉♊◐

20 Saturday

Black New Moon: Sydney: 01:53

♊◐

21 Sunday

♊◐

This Week

Although this month has hopefully been relatively painless, there are a few more challenging planetary alignments this week, so go easy on yourself and others.

27 May: First Quarter Moon

) What Are You Grateful For This Week? (

_____

_____

_____

_____

_____

_____

May – Week 21

22 Monday

♊ ♋ ●

_____

23 Tuesday

♋ ●

_____

24 Wednesday

♋ ♌ ◐

_____

25 Thursday

♌ ◐

_____

26 Friday

♌ ◐

_____

27 Saturday

First Quarter Moon

♌ ♍ ◐

28 Sunday

♍ ◐

_____

June

Full Moon: 3/4 June
Third Quarter Moon: 10 June
New Moon: 17/18 June
First Quarter Moon: 26 June

There are some extremely important astrological events happening this month, the most important of which is the move of the planet of passion and power, Pluto, back into the sign of Capricorn.

You may remember that back in March, Pluto moved into the sign of Aquarius. I mentioned that it would stay there until June. Well, here we are in June and Pluto has retrograded back in the sign of Capricorn for one last hurrah.

This really is this start of the end of an era. Pluto first entered the sign of Capricorn back in 2008, and now here we are in 2023 and this cycle is finally starting to end. Pluto will stay in Capricorn until January next year, when it'll move into Aquarius for a solid stay.

So what does this mean? So much!

For one thing, business is getting one last Plutonic blast. Pluto in Capricorn has seen businesses exploding and being rebuilt. It's been about trimming the fat from any businesses that had become too indulgent and carefree. It's been about ethics in business becoming an issue. It's been about governments being voted out or even brought down when needed.

On a personal level, wherever Pluto has been in your chart is where you've had a chance to have a thorough clear-out. Pluto gets rid of the dead wood so that transformation can take place. If you want to know which part of your chart Pluto is in between now and January 2024, take a look at the Full Moon in Capricorn 'How to Work with This Moon' section (see page 160).

This month I will:
- ❑ Detox my home
- ❑ Detox my relationships
- ❑ Detox my life

Full Moon in Sagittarius

KEY WORDS AND IDEAS FOR THIS LUNATION:

- Healing
- Freeing
- Adventurous
- Exciting

DATE AND TIME OF THIS MOON
London: 4 Jun, 04:41 | Sydney: 4 Jun, 13:41 | LA: 3 Jun, 20:41 | New York: 3 Jun, 23:41

Almost no sooner does June begin than we have the Full Moon in the sign of Sagittarius. As you may know, the Full Moon takes place when the Sun and the Moon are exactly opposite each other in the skies; in this case, the Sun is in Gemini and the Moon is in Sagittarius.

Some opposite signs really are opposites but with Gemini and Sagittarius, it's almost as though they have more in common than they have differences. Gemini loves to chat, in a chatterbox kind of way, while Sagittarius loves to expound and give lots of speeches, sometimes with a good dash of hot air. Gemini is always on the move; Sagittarius is all about travel. Gemini has a good mind; Sagittarius has a big mind. As you can see, these two signs blend well, so the Full Moon in Sagittarius is less confronting that others.

This Full Moon takes place at the time of a rather exciting Mercury–Uranus connection followed by a pretty sexy Venus–Pluto alignment. All in all, there is heat!

Breaking it down: Mercury and Uranus add up to the possibility, among other things, of an amazing conversation, a brainwave, or suddenly waking up to smell the coffee. Meanwhile, Venus–Pluto is great for the kind of romance that goes way beyond the superficial but also for power struggles in love and finances.

All in all, be sure to make time for your Forgiveness and Release practice... and b-r-e-a-t-h-e!

Seeing the Bigger Picture

While Gemini likes to think about every little thing, Sagittarius is about bigger ideas and the bigger picture. This Full Moon, make the most of this energy by completing the following exercise. If you're wrestling with more than one issue, you might like to do the exercise on a separate piece of paper for each one. Just complete the following:

I am worried that _____

_____

However, the bigger picture is that _____

_____

Therefore, I am grateful that _____

_____

How to Work with This Moon

To discover where the energy of this Full Moon is for you, find your Star sign or Rising sign here, see which House is involved, and then read 'A Quick Guide to the Houses' (see page 25): Aries – 9th House; Taurus – 8th House; Gemini – 7th House; Cancer – 6th House; Leo – 5th House; Virgo – 4th House; Libra – 3rd House; Scorpio – 2nd House; Sagittarius – 1st House; Capricorn – 12th House; Aquarius – 11th House; Pisces – 10th House.

QUESTIONS TO ASK AT THIS FULL MOON

This month, I'm changing things up a little for your Full Moon practice and we're going to focus on gratitude. Practising gratitude is one of the most important things any of us can do. Why? Because when we're grateful for the good things in our life we feel happier, and when we feel happier we attract even more to feel happy about. (It's the law of attraction at work!) You can still join me for a free Full Moon ritual via www.moonmessages.com/fbevents.

Who are the three people you're most grateful to have in your life, and why?

_____

_____

Which three places are you most grateful to have visited, and why?

_____

_____

_____

What are the three things in your life you're most grateful for, and why?

_____

_____

This Week

The meeting of Mercury and Uranus on 4 June could see people speaking out of turn, it's true. However, it's also amazing for brainstorming, so if you need some original ideas, brainstorm then!

3/4 June: Full Moon occurs at 13°Sg18'

☽ Affirmation of the Week ☾

'I release all criticism.'

LOUISE HAY

May/June – Week 22

29 Monday

_____ ♍♎ ◐

30 Tuesday

_____ ♎ ◐

31 Wednesday

_____ ♎♏ ◐

1 Thursday

_____ ♏ ◐

2 Friday

_____ ♏ ◐

3 Saturday

Full Moon: LA: 20:41 _____ ♏♐ ○

4 Sunday

Full Moon: London: 04:41 | Sydney: 13:41 | New York: 23:41 ♐ ○

This Week

The mighty move of passionate and powerful Pluto back into the sign of Capricorn, where it'll stay until January next year, happens on 11 June. This marks the beginning of the end of an astrological era that began in 2008 and will end in 2024.

5 June: Venus moves into Leo

10 June: Third Quarter Moon

11 June: Mercury moves into Gemini; Pluto retrograde moves into Capricorn

❨ What Are You Grateful For This Week? ❩

_____

_____

_____

_____

_____

June – Week 23

5 Monday

♐♑ ○

6 Tuesday

♑ ○

7 Wednesday

♑♒ ○

8 Thursday

♒ ◐

9 Friday

♒♓ ◑

10 Saturday

Third Quarter Moon

♓ ◑

11 Sunday

♓♈ ◑

New Moon in Gemini

KEY WORDS AND IDEAS FOR THIS LUNATION:

- Chatty
- Confusing
- Solid
- Lucky for some

DATE AND TIME OF THIS MOON

London: 18 Jun, 05:37 | Sydney: 18 Jun, 14:37 | LA: 17 Jun, 21:37 | New York: 18 Jun, 00:37

This looks like a mixed New Moon. On the one hand, it's in the sign of Gemini, so it's a great time to think about how you're thinking. For example, are you going hard with the negative self-talk? If so, stop! However, also note that this New Moon is clashing with the planet of confusion and deception, Neptune. So if you're not really too sure about anything at the time of the New Moon, that will be why.

Your best bet will be to meditate your way through the New Moon (depending on where you are in the world) and to just trust that everything is going to be fine.

Because of the Neptune clash and then the fact that the Moon goes Void of Course (meaning that it's transitioning from one zodiac sign to another), you might want to make your wishes 11 hours after the New Moon. It's not that the energies at the New Moon will be negative, but it's said what starts under a Void of Course Moon 'bears no fruit', so the energies will be better 11 hours later! You can refer to the times on the opposite page and then just add 11 hours to them for your New Moon ceremony. Or you can join me for my New Moon ritual via www.moonmessages.com/fbevents if you're so inclined!

Note that the day after the New Moon, we get one of the biggest and best astrological alignments of the year, as Jupiter harmonizes with Saturn. All the more reason to leave your wishes 11 hours after the New Moon to tap into this!

The Harder I Work, the Luckier I Get

One of my favourite quotes is from the father of musical impresario Andrew Lloyd Webber, who, when someone commented on how 'lucky' his son was to have done so well, reportedly replied, 'Yes, and the harder he works, the luckier he gets!' Are you someone who works hard but feel as though you don't get anywhere? This month, tap into the energies and ask yourself: *Where can I work smarter not harder?*

Write up your longer answer in your journal or elsewhere.

How to Work with This Moon

To discover where the energy of this New Moon is for you, find your Star sign or Rising sign here, see which House is involved, and then read 'A Quick Guide to the Houses' (see page 25): Aries –

3rd House; Taurus – 2nd House; Gemini – 1st House; Cancer – 12th House; Leo – 11th House; Virgo – 10th House; Libra – 9th House; Scorpio – 8th House; Sagittarius – 7th House; Capricorn – 6th House; Aquarius – 5th House; Pisces – 4th House.

NEW MOON WISHES AND INTENTIONS

My current biggest, most audacious goal, wish or intention is:

_____

_____

Now turn it into an affirmation. Write it here as if it's already happened and keep repeating it until the Full Moon.

_____

_____

Action steps I'm going to take towards this goal:

In the next 24 hours

_____

In the coming week

_____

In the month ahead

_____

Tip: Write these actions you can take in the diary.

I commit to this goal whole-heartedly!

Sign here:

_____

This Week

Don't let your thoughts get the better of you –
there is some astrological turbulence happening
mid-week, ahead of the New Moon.

17 June: Saturn goes retrograde (until 4 November 2023)

17/18 June: New Moon occurs at 26°Ge43'

☽ Affirmation of the Week ☾

'As I say yes to life,
life says yes to me.'

Louise Hay

June – Week 24

12 Monday

♈ ☽

13 Tuesday

♈ ♉ ☽

14 Wednesday

♉ ☽

15 Thursday

♉ ☽

16 Friday

♉ ♊ ☽

17 Saturday

New Moon: LA: 21:37

♊ ☽

18 Sunday

New Moon: London: 05:37 | Sydney: 14:37 | New York: 00:37

♊ ♋ ☽

This Week

It's a massive week as Jupiter harmonizes with Saturn. A great week to work hard on your dreams. Never give up! If you have a goal, it could be boosted this week.

19 June: Jupiter aligns with Saturn

21 June: the Sun moves into Cancer, marking the second Cardinal ingress of the year. Check into the Diary Bonuses area (www.moonmessages.com/diarybonuses2023) for your 'Reflect and Review' worksheet

21 June: Summer Solstice/Litha (northern hemisphere) and Winter Solstice/Yule (southern hemisphere)

❯ **What Are You Grateful For This Week?** ❮

_____

_____

_____

June – Week 25

19 Monday

_____

20 Tuesday

_____

21 Wednesday

_____

22 Thursday

_____

23 Friday

_____

24 Saturday

_____

25 Sunday

_____

This Week

It's a week for healing. That might mean getting some healing treatment, or it could be a conversation that proves to be healing. Focus on getting better, whatever ails you.

26 June: First Quarter Moon

27 June: Mercury moves into Cancer

30 June: Neptune goes retrograde (until 6 December 2023)

☽ What Are You Grateful For This Week? ☾

_____

_____

_____

_____

_____

_____

June/July – Week 26

26 Monday

First Quarter Moon _____ ♎ ◗

27 Tuesday

_____ ♎ ◗

28 Wednesday

_____ ♎ ♏ ◖

29 Thursday

_____ ♏ ◖

30 Friday

_____ ♏ ♐ ◯

1 Saturday

_____ ♐ ◯

2 Sunday

_____ ♐ ♑ ◯

July

Full Moon: 3 July
Third Quarter Moon: 10 July
New Moon: 17/18 July
First Quarter Moon: 25 July

Now is the time to be detoxing a part of your life that you know has gone toxic in some way. It's more than likely an area you've been wrestling with for many years. Use the relatively calm skies of this month to be honest about where you need to purge something from your life or where you know transformation is possible.

This month, there are no major dramas to contend with. As always, that doesn't mean life is going to be 100 per cent smooth sailing. Remember, we're here on Earth to evolve. There are always going to be challenges that take us up to the next level of consciousness. That said, this month there are no major clangs nor clashes.

Do be aware, though, that the start of the month sees a clash between Venus and Uranus. There could be some unexpected turns when it comes to love or money. Your best bet, if this happens to you, is to make 'Live and let live' your motto. Trying to control a situation or person is the last thing you should do at this point.

Also very important to note is the fact that on 23 July, the planet of love and abundance, Venus, starts one of her rare retrograde cycles – this time in the sign of Leo. Overall, it's a time to re-evaluate. If you have a partner, it can be a time when you feel quite disconnected from them; as though you're being given a chance to step back and think about what you and your partner have, especially if you've been taking each other for granted (don't do that!).

This month I will:
- ❏ Detox more
- ❏ Re-evaluate my life
- ❏ See through fakery

Full Moon in Capricorn

KEY WORDS AND IDEAS FOR THIS LUNATION:

- Transformative
- Releasing
- Lessons learned
- Work–life balance

DATE AND TIME OF THIS MOON

London: 3 Jul, 12:38 | Sydney: 3 Jul, 21:28 | LA: 3 Jul, 04:38 | New York: 3 Jul, 07:38

This is the last Full Moon in Capricorn we'll have this time around during the Pluto-in-Capricorn era. So what does that mean? It means it's time to tidy up your life wherever this Full Moon is activating your chart. So this month, as well as reading about the Full Moon in whatever part of your chart it's hitting, note that a detox is needed in this part of your life so that you can transform your life! Just refer back to 'A Quick Guide to the Houses' (see *page 25*) to see which House/part of your life this is all about.

> **Wherever this Full Moon is activating for you is where you need to detox, throw out the dead wood and make space for transformation. It's also where you need to look for a win-win situation in any struggles that are coming up now or between now and the end of this year.**

Another important question thrown out by this Full Moon is: do you have work–life balance? As Pluto has been moving through Capricorn since 2008 (and will continue to do until January next year), one of its messages has been about how we work – detoxing work on an individual level and at the level of companies and governments. If you know you work too hard, use this Full Moon to commit to paring things back so that you don't neglect your home life – we all need a balance!

This is a last-chance Full Moon so make sure you use it!

Heart and Mind

What you'll need: a (preferably black) candle; a pen and paper; laurel essential oil (optional). Put on some beautiful music (I love www.edoandjo.com and Deva Premal) and fire up your essential oil burner.

Ask yourself: where have you been allowing your head to rule your heart, logic to override your emotions, or fears to rule out intuition? Write your answers on a piece of paper and then burn it while saying, 'I am releasing all negativity that stops me from connecting with who I really am.' Plant the ashes of the paper in your garden or in a pot plant.

How to Work with This Moon

To discover where the energy of this Full Moon is for you, find your Star sign or Rising sign here, see which House is involved, and then read 'A Quick Guide to the Houses' (see page 25): Aries – 10th House; Taurus – 9th House; Gemini – 8th House; Cancer – 7th House; Leo – 6th House; Virgo – 5th House; Libra – 4th House; Scorpio – 3rd House; Sagittarius – 2nd House; Capricorn – 1st House; Aquarius – 12th House; Pisces – 11th House.

FULL MOON FORGIVENESS AND QUESTIONS TO ASK

This Full Moon also asks us to get real about our feelings. Remember, feelings have the power to create. So if you know you've been having bad feelings about something, honour those feelings — but by the same token, if you know those feelings are definitely fear-driven, then release them. Join me for a free Full Moon ritual via www.moonmessages. com/fbevents.

I forgive/release:

_____

_____

Thinking about my biggest fear: is it real or is it pure nonsense — and why?

_____

_____

If it's nonsense, what steps can I take to start to release this fear?

_____

_____

How would my life look if I released this fear?

_____

_____

This Week

If you have an upset with someone this week, try to breathe through it. There is some quite argumentative energy this week, followed by kinder, 'kiss-and-make-up' vibes.

3 July: Full Moon occurs at 11°Cp18'

) Affirmation of the Week (

'I release all drama
from my life.'

LOUISE HAY

July – Week 27

3 Monday

Full Moon: London: 12:38 | Sydney: 21:28 | LA: 04:38 | New York: 07:38

4 Tuesday

5 Wednesday

6 Thursday

7 Friday

8 Saturday

9 Sunday

This Week

If you have nothing better to do this week, use the energies of Mars moving into Virgo by giving your home and office a good clear-out!

10 July: Third Quarter Moon; Mars moves into Virgo

11 July: Mercury moves into Leo

☽ What Are You Grateful For This Week? ☾

July – Week 28

10 Monday

Third Quarter Moon

11 Tuesday

12 Wednesday

13 Thursday

14 Friday

15 Saturday

16 Sunday

New Moon in Cancer

KEY WORDS AND IDEAS FOR THIS LUNATION:

- Powerful
- Power struggles
- The Feminine Rising
- Dreams coming true

DATE AND TIME OF THIS MOON
London: 17 Jul, 19:31 | Sydney: 18 Jul, 04:31 | LA: 17 Jul, 11:31 | New York: 17 Jul, 14:31

There is a such a lot to unpack in this powerful New Moon in the sign of Cancer, which is not only one of the Moon's home signs, but also a sign of the Divine Feminine.

If you're using this diary, it's likely that on some level you already understand that the Divine Feminine is finally rising again. In 2021, I interviewed my fellow astrologer Demetra George, who put forward a very good case for the idea that 5,000 years ago, when the patriarchy took over, the Goddess and the Divine Feminine were not abolished and didn't disappear, but went into a kind of abeyance or hiding, just as the Moon does during her Dark Moon phase before the New Moon. As Demetra put it: '[We saw] the withdrawal of the Goddess into her hidden phase, because that's where she does her mysteries of renewal – it's is a normal and natural part of every cycle.'

That was 5,000 years ago, and many believe we're now at the start of the re-emergence of the Divine Feminine and the Goddess.

Every New and Full Moon is a time to celebrate, but the New Moon in Cancer is an especially good time. And this 2023 New Moon in Cancer – opposite Pluto, the planet of life, death and rebirth – is especially a time to celebrate the Feminine.

One of the best ways to make the most of these energies is to meditate on whatever you want to transform in your life.

Ideas for Celebrating This New Moon

- Get together with your most magical female friend(s) and do your New Moon wishing and intention-setting together.

- Write a letter to your mother or to the woman who has most influenced your life in a positive way.

- Spend time alone in quiet meditation just after the New Moon and ask the Goddess for a message. Write it down.

- Commit to a new or more regular meditation practice. Try listening to solfeggio frequencies on your headphones if you have trouble sitting still.

- Create a vision board of your dreams.

How to Work with This Moon

To discover where the energy of this New Moon is for you, find your Star sign or Rising sign here, see which House is involved, and then read 'A Quick Guide to the Houses' (see *page 25*): Aries – 4th House; Taurus – 3rd House; Gemini – 2nd House; Cancer – 1st House; Leo – 12th House; Virgo – 11th House; Libra – 10th House; Scorpio – 9th House; Sagittarius – 8th House; Capricorn – 7th House; Aquarius – 6th House; Pisces – 5th House.

NEW MOON WISHES AND INTENTIONS

My current biggest, most audacious goal, wish or intention is:

_____

_____

Now turn it into an affirmation. Write it here as if it's already happened and keep repeating it until the Full Moon.

_____

_____

Action steps I'm going to take towards this goal:

In the next 24 hours

_____

In the coming week

_____

In the month ahead

_____

Tip: Write these actions you can take in the diary.

I commit to this goal whole-heartedly!

Sign here:

_____

This Week

If you know you're wasting your energy on someone or something, this is the week to get real and ask yourself whether you really want this to go on.

17/18 July: New Moon occurs at 24°Cn56'

23 July: Venus goes retrograde; the Sun moves into Leo

☽ Affirmation of the Week ☾

'I welcome miracles
into my life.'

LOUISE HAY

July – Week 29

17 Monday

New Moon: London: 19:31 | LA: 11:31 | New York: 14:31

18 Tuesday

New Moon: Sydney: 04:31

19 Wednesday

20 Thursday

21 Friday

22 Saturday

23 Sunday

This Week

A wonderful week to let someone know how you feel, especially if you know you should have said something a little bit earlier, as communications planet Mercury connects with retrograde Venus.

25 July: First Quarter Moon

28 July: Mercury moves into Virgo

☽ What Are You Grateful For This Week? ☾

July – Week 30

24 Monday

♎ ◖

25 Tuesday

First Quarter Moon   ♎ ♏ ◑

26 Wednesday

♏ ◑

27 Thursday

♏ ◑

28 Friday

♏ ♐ ◐

29 Saturday

♐ ◐

30 Sunday

♐ ♑ ◐

August

Full Moon: 1/2 August
Third Quarter Moon: 8 August
New Moon: 16 August
First Quarter Moon: 24 August
Full Moon: 30/31 August

As August dawns, the skies are what you could call pretty darned benign. Yes, there are some tense alignments ahead but they are all between the faster-moving planets. This means that they might feel like bumps in the road, but overall will pass quite quickly.

The basic rule of thumb with the August alignments is this: do live and let live and do allow life to unfold, but don't go too far, don't exaggerate, don't go OTT, avoid trying to control anyone, don't overspend, don't let your ego go crazy and avoid anyone who's trying to boss you around.

This month we get one New Moon and two Full Moons! These come in this order: Full Moon in Aquarius, New Moon in Leo, Full Moon in Pisces. Moreover, the first Full Moon is also a Super Full Moon (and therefore will appear 14 per cent larger and 40 per cent brighter to us), while the second Full Moon is also known as a Blue Full Moon (because it's the second Full Moon in single calendar month).

So this month has double the chances to do Full Moon work, which means it has double the chances to let something go, which means it has double the chances of helping you to break free from the past so that you're better able to be in the present to create your future.

Also note that the planet of love and abundance, Venus, is retrograde. This only happens about once every 18 months. Venus is about values – among other things – so it's a very good time to re-evaluate everything. For some, it's the ideal time to reunite with an ex-partner, too, or to finally get proper closure.

This month I will:
❑ Spend wisely
❑ Live and let live
❑ Breathe through dramas

Super Full Moon
in Aquarius

**KEY WORDS AND IDEAS
FOR THIS LUNATION:**

- Speak your truth
- Slow down
- Make an effort
- Try your luck

DATE AND TIME OF THIS MOON
London: 1 Aug, 19:31 | Sydney: 2 Aug, 04:31 | LA: 1 Aug, 11:31 | New York: 1 Aug, 14:31

This Full Moon is the first of two Full Moons in August and it's a Supermoon (a New or Full Moon that closely coincides with perigee – the Moon's closest point to Earth in her monthly orbit). There are four to six Supermoons a year and, although they have no real astrological significance, people tend to get quite excited about them – not least because the Moon appears so much bigger and brighter in the sky. They are perhaps more impactful if they affect your own personal Moon on your birth chart. (To find that out you need to know your chart, which you can find for free at www. moonmessages.com/freechart.) All in all, this Full Moon has a lot going for it!

At the time of the Full Moon, Mercury will be making an opposition to Saturn, so it's the perfect time to speak your mind, say your piece or have that hard conversation.

Do focus on speaking your truth while not hurting the feelings of the person you're talking too. Don't let anyone bully you now.

If someone you're speaking to makes you feel bad, use some humour to diffuse the situation. There is also a lovely Mars–Jupiter alignment taking place around the time of this Full Moon, which should lighten the mood considerably.

Note that love and abundance planet, Venus, is still retrograde at the time of this Full Moon. That means it's still the time to weigh up what really matters in your life. Don't be too proud to let someone know if they matter to you and you haven't been showing it!

Fire and Ice

At the time of the Full Moon, find somewhere you can light a small fire. I have a little metal portable fire pit that I use, but a ceramic fireproof dish works equally well, for example. Have some ice on standby.

Light the fire and, once it's burning, put the ice on a plate and speak onto it, telling it everything that you're letting go. Imagine your words falling onto the ice and imprinting it. Then either hold the plate of ice near the fire so that the ice melts, or actually slide the ice onto the fire itself. Visualize the words dissolving as the ice melts away.

How to Work with This Moon

To discover where the energy of this Full Moon is for you, find your Star sign or Rising sign here, see which House is involved, and then read 'A Quick Guide to the Houses' (see page 25): Aries – 11th House; Taurus – 10th House; Gemini – 9th House; Cancer – 8th House; Leo – 7th House; Virgo – 6th House; Libra – 5th House; Scorpio – 4th House; Sagittarius – 3rd House; Capricorn – 2nd House; Aquarius – 1st House; Pisces – 12th House.

FULL MOON FORGIVENESS AND QUESTIONS TO ASK

So what are you releasing this month? Remember, August brings double the chances to release and let go. The Full Moon in Aquarius is great because the Aquarius energy is quite detached, so it's easier to let go of whatever you know you need to. Write your list below, tear out the page, and then burn it. Join me for a free Full Moon ritual via www.moonmessages.com/fbevents.

I forgive/release:

_____

_____

_____

_____

What lessons have I learned recently?

_____

How will life be different because of these lessons?

_____

Am I working on keeping my thoughts positive – and if not, how is that affecting me? Can I change?

_____

This Week

The main challenge this Full Moon week, as Mercury opposes Saturn, is to keep your thoughts positive. Train your brain — leave behind negativity.

1 August: festivals of Lammas (northern hemisphere) and Imbolc (southern hemisphere)

1/2 August: Super Full Moon occurs at 09°Aq15'

) Affirmation of the Week (

'I trust the process of life.'

LOUISE HAY

July/August – Week 31

31 Monday

♑ ○

1 Tuesday

Super Full Moon: London: 19:31 | LA: 11:31 | New York: 14:31

♑ ♒ ○

2 Wednesday

Super Full Moon: Sydney: 04:31

♒ ○

3 Thursday

♒ ♓ ○

4 Friday

♓ ○

5 Saturday

♓ ♈ ○

6 Sunday

♈ ○

This Week

There could be some unexpected curveballs to do with love or abundance this week, but it really does look like a case of all's well that ends well.

8 August: Third Quarter Moon

) What Are You Grateful For This Week? (

_____

_____

_____

_____

_____

_____

_____

August – Week 32

7 Monday

8 Tuesday

Third Quarter Moon

9 Wednesday

10 Thursday

11 Friday

12 Saturday

13 Sunday

New Moon
in Leo

KEY WORDS AND IDEAS
FOR THIS LUNATION:

- Destiny calling
- Take action
- Efforts pay off
- Shine

DATE AND TIME OF THIS MOON

London: 16 Aug, 10:38 | Sydney: 16 Aug, 19:38 | LA: 16 Aug, 02:38 | New York: 16 Aug, 05:38

It could be a bit of a bumpy ride up to this New Moon. If you like to work with the Dark Moon, then make sure you do it this month. The Dark Moon is a not-strictly-astrological phase that takes place just before the New Moon. It's the perfect time to let anything and everything crumble away. What do you need to release? In the day or two before the New Moon, take some time to make a note of what you're releasing. Breathe it out. Write it down and burn it. Or join me via www.moonmessages.com/fbevents for a free ceremony.

The good news is that once we get through this Dark Moon, the energy is far more positive.

> For one thing, this New Moon is taking place in the shiny sign of Leo. That's already a good thing because Leo is a sign that loves to live large and we'll all feel it, regardless of which sign we actually are.

Moreover, shortly after the New Moon, the Sun will be making a harmonious aspect to the auspicious north node. For many there is a shared sense that destiny is calling.

We may be getting towards the end of the calendar year now, but remember that calendars are just man-made frameworks. This could be the start of a whole new cycle for you. Embrace it!

Again, as with the most recent Full Moon, note that loving and abundant Venus is still in one of her rare retrograde cycles. It's time to reconsider what matters most to you – and soon it will be time to take action on that. Don't let pride trip you up.

Oh, Fabulous You!

Leo is the sign of showbusiness, glamour and razzmatazz. It's the sign that thinks it's fabulous as it takes centre stage. And we all have Leo in our chart somewhere. This lunation, take a moment to note down three things that you know are fabulous about you.

1. _____

2. _____

3. _____

How to Work with This Moon

To discover where the energy of this New Moon is for you, find your Star sign or Rising sign here, see which House is involved, and then read 'A Quick Guide to the Houses' (see page 25): Aries – 5th House; Taurus – 4th House; Gemini – 3rd House; Cancer – 2nd House; Leo – 1st House; Virgo – 12th House; Libra – 11th House; Scorpio – 10th House; Sagittarius – 9th House; Capricorn – 8th House; Aquarius – 7th House; Pisces – 6th House.

NEW MOON WISHES AND INTENTIONS

My current biggest, most audacious goal, wish or intention is:

_____

_____

Now turn it into an affirmation. Write it here as if it's already happened and keep repeating it until the Full Moon.

_____

_____

Action steps I'm going to take towards this goal:

In the next 24 hours

_____

In the coming week

_____

In the month ahead

_____

Tip: Write these actions you can take in the diary.

I commit to this goal whole-heartedly!

Sign here:

_____

This Week

There is so much going on at the time of this week's
New Moon in Leo. Life could happen very fast
and very nicely. Get clear on your desires.

16 August: New Moon occurs at 23°Le17'

❭ Affirmation of the Week ❰

'Whatever I need to know is revealed to
me at exactly the right time.'

Louise Hay

August – Week 33

14 Monday

_____

15 Tuesday

_____

16 Wednesday

New Moon: London: 10:38 | Sydney: 19:38 | LA: 02:38 | New York: 05:38
_____

17 Thursday

_____

18 Friday

_____

19 Saturday

_____

20 Sunday

_____

This Week

Mercury goes retrograde this week. This time around it's doing it in the detail-oriented sign of Virgo, so this could be quite an intense retrograde cycle for us all!

23 August: the Sun moves into Virgo; Mercury goes retrograde (until 15 September)

24 August: First Quarter Moon

27 August: Mars moves into Libra

 **What Are You Grateful For This Week?**

August – Week 34

21 Monday

♎ ♏ ●

22 Tuesday

♏ ◗

23 Wednesday

♏ ◑

24 Thursday

First Quarter Moon

♏ ♐ ◑

25 Friday

♐ ◐

26 Saturday

♐ ♑ ◐

27 Sunday

♑ ◯

Blue Super Full Moon in Pisces

KEY WORDS AND IDEAS FOR THIS LUNATION:

- Lucky for some
- Dreamy
- Opportunities opening
- Second chances

DATE AND TIME OF THIS MOON

London: 31 Aug, 02:35 | Sydney: 31 Aug, 11:35 | LA: 30 Aug, 18:35 | New York: 30 Aug, 21:35

This second Full Moon in August (hence the name 'Blue Moon') is taking place in the dreamy sign of Pisces. It's also making a harmonious aspect to the Pisces ruler, Jupiter. Full Moons tend to be unbalanced, rather intense times. Here's the thing: the Moon represents our emotions in astrology, and as She swells to fullness each month – or twice in one month, as is the case this month – our emotions swell too. However, how it feels to us here on Earth depends on the condition of the Full Moon from one month to the next.

All in all, this augurs well for the energies around the time of this Full Moon.

> **Remember that Pisces is a very psychic sign. Tap into the numinous energies with some good old-fashioned divination.**

Consider me biased, but my favourite way to tap into the energies and to practise divination is using Oracle cards. In case you didn't know, I have two decks: Moonology™ Oracle Cards and Moonology™ Manifestation Oracle Cards. Whichever cards you have, pull them out now. Meditate and then ask your most pressing question.

As this Full Moon takes place, the planet of communication – Mercury – is retrograde. You may find that emotional issues from the past are coming up again. Maybe you didn't deal with them very well last time, and can do better this time?

Note that Pisces is the last of the 12 zodiac signs. So if you committed to working with all 12 Full Moons the past 12 months, well done! You've reached the end of that cycle – all the better to start a new one next month!

Where Are You?

As already noted, this Full Moon is the last in the full cycle of 12 through the zodiac. Take a moment now to think about the last 12 months. What have you achieved and what have you moved on from successfully? How different do you feel now compared with how you felt a year ago? Give yourself a pat on the back where you know you've achieved something substantial. If you're still not where you want to be, don't be hard on yourself. Be gentle with yourself and just keep going. Life goes in cycles and we'll be starting a new Full Moon cycle next month.

How to Work with This Moon

To discover where the energy of this Full Moon is for you, find your Star sign or Rising sign here, see which House is involved, and then read 'A Quick Guide to the Houses' (see page 25): Aries – 12th House; Taurus – 11th House; Gemini – 10th House; Cancer – 9th House; Leo – 8th House; Virgo – 7th House; Libra – 6th House; Scorpio – 5th House; Sagittarius – 4th House; Capricorn – 3rd House; Aquarius – 2nd House; Pisces – 1st House.

FULL MOON FORGIVENESS
AND QUESTIONS TO ASK

This is a pretty important Full Moon to work with because it's the last of the current cycle, before we start a new Full Moon cycle next month with the Full Moon in Aries. Think of it like a basket into which you can dump everything you want to leave behind. Write it all down. Don't leave anything out. Join me for a free Full Moon ritual via www.moonmessages.com/fbevents.

I forgive/release:

_____

_____

_____

_____

Thinking about your psychic abilities, which one would you most like to develop and are you willing to put in the effort?

_____

In what ways do you feel most lucky?

_____

Are you willing to leave the past behind and how do you think that will affect your life?

_____

This Week

A very lovely Full Moon in Pisces augurs extremely well for a peaceful and even uplifting Full Moon experience.

29 August: Uranus retrograde begins

30/31 August: Blue Super Full Moon occurs at 07°Pi25'

❯ Affirmation of the Week ❮

'I am deeply fulfilled
by all that I do.'

LOUISE HAY

August/September – Week 35

28 Monday

♑♒ ◯

29 Tuesday

♒ ◯

30 Wednesday

Blue Super Full Moon: LA: 18:35 | New York: 21:35

♒♓ ◯

31 Thursday

Blue Super Full Moon: London: 02:35 | Sydney: 11:35

♓ ◯

1 Friday

♓♈ ◯

2 Saturday

♈ ◯

3 Sunday

♈♉ ◯

September

The first thing to know this month is that if you and your partner have been having issues or feeling somehow 'apart', or if you've been weighing up your life and you're not sure what to think or feel, all that should start to ease up now.

Venus, the planet of love, relationships, values and self-esteem (among other things), has been in a rare retrograde cycle that finishes very early this month. As with any retrograde, the start and the end of the cycle are always felt most strongly. So if you've been experiencing some of these feelings as September begins, just breathe through them and allow yourself time to digest everything.

Meanwhile, Mercury also ends its retrograde cycle. Since it was in detail-loving Virgo, this retrograde may have been quite discombobulating for some. If that includes you, relief is coming!

The ideal outcome from any Mercury retrograde cycle – no matter which sign it's in and no matter which sign you are – is to rethink, revisit and revise something important to you. As we come to the end of the retrograde cycle on 15 September, don't make any sudden decisions. Allow yourself to digest all the information that's come in during the past few weeks before you take action.

As we move towards the end of September, the Sun moves into the sign of Libra. Libra is the sign of relationships, so when the Sun is in this sign every year, it's a really good time to think about how well you're relating to others.

This month I will:
- ❏ Take time to make decisions
- ❏ Decide what I really value
- ❏ Work on my relationships

This Week

The energies around communications planet Mercury (still retrograde) are very good this week. It should be a very good time to have an important conversation you needed earlier or that relates to the past.

4 September: Venus retrograde ends; Jupiter goes retrograde (until 24 December 2023)

6 September: Third Quarter Moon

❯ What Are You Grateful For This Week? ❮

_____

_____

_____

_____

_____

September – Week 36

4 Monday

♉○

5 Tuesday

♉♊◑

6 Wednesday

Third Quarter Moon   ♊◑

7 Thursday

♊◐

8 Friday

♊♋◐

9 Saturday

♋◐

10 Sunday

♋♌◐

New Moon in Virgo

KEY WORDS AND IDEAS FOR THIS LUNATION:

- Expect changes
- Take care of business
- Get organized
- Break free

DATE AND TIME OF THIS MOON

London: 15 Sep, 02:39 | Sydney: 15 Sep, 11:39 | LA: 14 Sep, 18:39 | New York: 14 Sep, 21:39

This is a powerful New Moon. For a start, the ruler of the New Moon is the planet Mercury and it's stationing at the time of the New Moon – that means it's shifting from being retrograde to going forwards again.

This New Moon, you might sense that it's time to make your mind up about something – although perhaps give it a week or two before you make any bold decisions.

Meanwhile, the mild New Moon in Virgo is being totally emboldened by its tight alignment with the planet of chaos, change, awakenings and liberation, Uranus. The effect of this energy is to make it easier to get things moving. It's going to be more possible than usual to move things forwards. What in your life do you need to get on with? Use the energy of the New Moon. It's a bit like a cube of ice sliding down a hot silver surface: the more it melts, the faster it goes. That's pretty much the message for this New Moon: where do you need to get a wriggle on, as they say?

This New Moon is also making what's known as a Grand Trine with the planets Uranus and Pluto. This truly augurs very well for making liberating transformations in your life. Tap in with your own New Moon ritual or join me on Facebook (see www.moonmessages. com/fbevents).

What Do You Really Value?

This New Moon comes about 10 days after the end of the Venus retrograde cycle, which should have allowed you enough time to digest all the feelings it brought up. Tap into the wisdom of this recent cycle by making a list below of the five people or situations you value most. Are you living your life with these values as your priority?

1. _____

2. _____

3. _____

4. _____

5. _____

How to Work with This Moon

To discover where the energy of this New Moon is for you, find your Star sign or Rising sign here, see which House is involved, and then read 'A Quick Guide to the Houses' (see page 25): Aries – 6th House; Taurus – 5th House; Gemini – 4th House; Cancer – 3rd House; Leo – 2nd House; Virgo – 1st House; Libra – 12th House; Scorpio – 11th House; Sagittarius – 10th House; Capricorn – 9th House; Aquarius – 8th House; Pisces – 7th House.

NEW MOON WISHES AND INTENTIONS

My current biggest, most audacious goal, wish or intention is:

_____

_____

Now turn it into an affirmation. Write it here as if it's already happened and keep repeating it until the Full Moon.

_____

_____

Action steps I'm going to take towards this goal:

In the next 24 hours

_____

In the coming week

_____

In the month ahead

_____

Tip: Write these actions you can take in the diary.

I commit to this goal whole-heartedly!

Sign here:

_____

This Week

Mercury goes direct (ends its retrograde cycle) towards the end of the week. Remember that the start or end of a retrograde cycle can be the most intense, so allow room for mix-ups.

14/15 September: New Moon occurs at 21°Vi58'

15 September: Mercury retrograde ends

❫ Affirmation of the Week ❪

'I am loved,
and I am at peace.'

LOUISE HAY

September – Week 37

11 Monday

♌

12 Tuesday

♌

13 Wednesday

♌ ♍

14 Thursday

New Moon: LA: 18:39 | New York: 21:39

♍

15 Friday

New Moon: London: 02:39 | Sydney: 11:39

♍ ♎

16 Saturday

♎

17 Sunday

♎

This Week

Both 19 and 20 September have really powerful
energies. Even if you already did your New Moon wishes,
boost them now by sitting down and taking a good
15 minutes or so to do some creative visualization.

23 September: the Sun moves into Libra, marking
the third Cardinal ingress of the year. Check into
the Diary Bonuses area (www.moonmessages.com/
diarybonuses2023) for your 'Reflect and Review' worksheet

22 September: First Quarter Moon

23 September: Autumn Equinox/Mabon (northern hemisphere)
and Spring Equinox/Ostara (southern hemisphere)

❱ What Are You Grateful For This Week? ❰

_____

_____

_____

September – Week 38

18 Monday

♎ ♏ ♐ ◐

19 Tuesday

♏ ♐ ◐

20 Wednesday

♏ ♐ ♐ ◑

21 Thursday

♐ ◑

22 Friday

First Quarter Moon

♐ ♑ ◑

23 Saturday

♑ ◑

24 Sunday

♑ ♒ ◑

Full Moon
in Aries

KEY WORDS AND IDEAS
FOR THIS LUNATION:

- Starting over
- Acting wildly!
- Fiery
- You versus me

DATE AND TIME OF THIS MOON

London: 29 Sep, 10:57 | Sydney: 29 Sep, 19:57 | LA: 29 Sep, 02:57 | New York: 29 Sep, 05:57

Hang on to your hats, because this could be one heck of a Full Moon! For a start, it's taking place in the first sign of the zodiac, Aries. Aries is ruled by the planet of fire and anger, Mars. It's the baby of the zodiac, and always puts itself first. Gentle reminder: we all have Aries in our chart somewhere! It's where we're on fire. (You can find out where it is in your chart for free at www.moonmessages. com/freechart). But wait, there's more:

> **At the time of this Full Moon, the planet of love and abundance, Venus, is clashing with the planet of chaos and unpredictability, Uranus, so all bets are off when it comes to saying exactly how everything is going to play out.**

But we can bet it's going to be possibly a little bit jarring, hopefully exciting (in a really good way), and maybe even quite liberating for those of us who've got the courage to just go for it in terms of whatever we want. Do you feel a need to liberate yourself from someone or something? That urge could really grow now.

Also note that, if you're just picking up the diary for the first time now, it's still worth engaging at this point. Yes, you've missed a few months! However, this is the first Full Moon in the sign of Aries, which means we're at the start of a new 12-month cycle. Commit to working with every Full Moon from now until this time next year and you'll change your life for the better. How do I know? Because I've done it myself and so have thousands of my students and readers.

Are You Committed to Your Personal Growth?

This month, I'm going to ask you to go within yourself. Are you really willing to change your life so that you can live the life of your dreams? As humans, we all have that as our birthright, but that's not always easy to believe. If you're willing to commit to creating your best life, sign this pledge below.

I, _____ , do hereby commit to working with each and every Full Moon in the coming 12 months.

How to Work with This Moon

To discover where the energy of this Full Moon is for you, find your Star sign or Rising sign here, see which House is involved, and then read

'A Quick Guide to the Houses' (see page 25): Aries – 1st House; Taurus – 12th House; Gemini – 11th House; Cancer – 10th House; Leo – 9th House; Virgo – 8th House; Libra – 7th House; Scorpio – 6th House; Sagittarius – 5th House; Capricorn – 4th House; Aquarius – 3rd House; Pisces – 2nd House.

FULL MOON FORGIVENESS AND QUESTIONS TO ASK

Luckily, the thunder-and-lightning aspect of this Full Moon lends itself to more intense emotions, which in turn lend themselves to more powerful work. Feel all your feelings fully. Let them swirl like a maelstrom in your body. And then release them via forgiveness and just good, old-fashioned 'letting go'. Join me for a free Full Moon ritual via www.moonmessages.com/fbevents.

I forgive/release:

_____

_____

_____

_____

Where in my life do I feel trapped, and what am I going to do about it?

Have I been blaming someone for the way I am? If so, who is that person, and why have I been blaming them?

_____

How can I stop blaming others for where I am in life today? (Therein lies liberation.)

_____

This Week

It's possible that things could swirl out of control a bit now – the energies are a bit crazy! However, the good news is that a rather lovely Mercury–Uranus link now means that one good conversation could sort everything out.

29 September: Full Moon occurs at 06°Ar00'

☽ Affirmation of the Week ☾

'As I forgive myself,
it becomes easier to forgive others.'

LOUISE HAY

September/October – Week 39

25 Monday

26 Tuesday

27 Wednesday

28 Thursday

29 Friday

Full Moon: London: 10:57 | Sydney: 19:57 | LA: 02:57 | New York: 05:57

30 Saturday

1 Sunday

October

Third Quarter Moon: 6 October
New Moon: 14/15 October
First Quarter Moon: 22 October
Full Moon: 28/29 October

The past few months have been relatively quiet, astrologically speaking, even if they've been a wild ride as far as Moon energies are concerned. Hopefully you've been pretty much cruising through life too. Of course, that depends on what's going on in your personal chart. If you've been up and down, then this month is perhaps going to be the turning point you need.

October brings not one but two eclipses. Eclipses, remember, are like portals to another life. If you're not happy with where you are, they are like a sliding door that you can walk through to another way of being. Eclipses are only difficult when we absolutely resist the change that our soul knows we need. They put us back on our right and proper path and are super-powerful to work with.

Also worth noting this month is that the planet of power and passion, Pluto, is resuming direct motion, as we say in astrology. In other words, it's completed its latest retrograde cycle and will now start moving forwards again.

Pluto is getting closer to the end of its stay in the sign of Capricorn, so we're nearing the last chance to detox our lives in whichever part of our chart we have Capricorn. To verify where that is, take a look at the House that's being activated by the Full Moon in Capricorn (*see page 160*). That's the same House that Pluto is in for you.

Pluto will move into Aquarius in January next year, it'll make a brief and final foray into Capricorn once more in September 2024 and then it'll finally move into Aquarius until January 2044.

This month I will:
❑ Start something new
❑ Leave something behind
❑ Rise like a phoenix!

This Week

If you need to convince someone of something, this is a very good week to state your case, thanks to a highly persuasive link between Mercury and Pluto.

5 October: Mercury moves into Libra

6 October: Third Quarter Moon

☽ What Are You Grateful For This Week? ☾

October – Week 40

2 Monday

_____

3 Tuesday

_____

4 Wednesday

_____

5 Thursday

_____

6 Friday

Third Quarter Moon

_____

7 Saturday

_____

8 Sunday

_____

New Moon Eclipse in Libra

KEY WORDS AND IDEAS FOR THIS LUNATION:

- Power struggles
- More detoxing
- Relationship reset
- Luck in love

DATE AND TIME OF THIS MOON

London: 14 Oct, 18:55 | Sydney: 15 Oct, 04:55 | LA: 14 Oct, 10:55 | New York: 14 Oct, 13:55

All New Moon eclipses pack a powerful punch. As explained earlier, they are like a sliding door that we can walk through to another way of being. Back in the olden days, people feared eclipses, because they took everyone by surprise. No one then knew why the sky went dark, but today we know that they're caused by a total eclipse of the Sun.

When I was first learning astrology, I had a pretty serious eclipse on my Sun while Saturn went over my Venus – painful. If you don't know much about astrology and this all sounds very complicated, please don't worry about it! All you need to know is that what happened at that eclipse was quite painful but led to the happiest days of my life. That's how eclipses are a lot of the time. In my case, I broke out of a terribly toxic relationship and very soon afterwards met my beloved husband. Had I stayed in that toxic relationship, none of that would have happened.

> Eclipses are often about the nasty things you just don't want to face. Your soul wants you to face them so you can extricate yourself and move on to something better.

Not every eclipse will hit you as strongly as that one hit me. But be open to changing your life now as we move towards the Moon eclipse in the sign of Libra, which is all about relationships.

Create Your Future

It's time to draw up your future, as we experience the New Moon eclipse. Grab some paper and coloured pens or pencils and draw a large noughts-and-crosses grid. In each square of the grid write words such as: love, money, travel, family, work, fun, spirituality, friends, and so on. Now imagine what you want in each of these parts of your life, picture it in your mind's eye, and then – *even if you do laughable stick figures* – draw in what you want for yourself in that part of your life.

This is my preferred method for this exercise, but you could also rip pictures out of magazines or download images from the Internet to show your desires if you prefer.

How to Work with This Moon

To discover where the energy of this New Moon is for you, find your Star sign or Rising sign here, see which House is involved, and then read 'A Quick Guide to the Houses' (*see page 25*): Aries – 7th House; Taurus – 6th House; Gemini – 5th House; Cancer – 4th House; Leo – 3rd House; Virgo – 2nd House; Libra – 1st House; Scorpio – 12th House; Sagittarius – 11th House; Capricorn – 10th House; Aquarius – 9th House; Pisces – 8th House.

NEW MOON WISHES AND INTENTIONS

My current biggest, most audacious goal, wish or intention is:

_____

_____

Now turn it into an affirmation. Write it here as if it's already happened and keep repeating it until the Full Moon.

_____

_____

Action steps I'm going to take towards this goal:

In the next 24 hours

_____

In the coming week

_____

In the month ahead

_____

Tip: Write these actions you can take in the diary.

I commit to this goal whole-heartedly!

Sign here:

_____

This Week

It's a New Moon eclipse week. This is one of the most powerful, energetic times of the entire year. Make sure you do your New Moon wishes and intentions. Really spend time on them.

9 October: Venus moves into Virgo

11 October: Pluto retrograde ends

12 October: Mars moves into Scorpio

14/15 October: New Moon eclipse occurs at 21°Li07'

) Affirmation of the Week (

'My happy thoughts help create
my healthy body.'

Louise Hay

October – Week 41

9 Monday

♌ ☽

10 Tuesday

♌ ♍ ☽

11 Wednesday

♍ ☽

12 Thursday

♍ ☽

13 Friday

♍ ♎ ☽

14 Saturday

New Moon eclipse: London: 18:55 | LA: 10:55 | New York: 13:55

♎ ☽

15 Sunday

New Moon eclipse: Sydney: 04:55

♎ ♏ ☽

This Week

Passionate and sometimes paranoid Pluto is being activated this week. If you find yourself in a power struggle, disengage and look for a win-win resolution.

22 October: First Quarter Moon; Mercury moves into Scorpio

☽ What Are You Grateful For This Week? ☾

_____

_____

_____

_____

_____

_____

_____

October – Week 42

16 Monday

♏︎

17 Tuesday

♏︎ ♐︎

18 Wednesday

♐︎

19 Thursday

♐︎

20 Friday

♐︎ ♑︎

21 Saturday

♑︎

22 Sunday

First Quarter Moon

♑︎ ♒︎

Full Moon
Eclipse in Taurus

KEY WORDS AND IDEAS
FOR THIS LUNATION:

- Lucky for some
  - Chatty
- Changeable
  - Defining

DATE AND TIME OF THIS MOON

London: 28 Oct, 21:24 | Sydney: 29 Oct, 07:24 | LA: 28 Oct, 13:24 | New York: 28 Oct, 16:24

This really is a Full Moon eclipse of many colours! Full Moon eclipses can be really tricky, because they demand that we let go and move on from something we've been clinging on to that's no longer in our best interest. Obviously, that can be a pretty difficult experience at times. This Full Moon eclipse is taking place near communications planet Mercury and the lucky planet Jupiter.

So, on the one hand, there is a big risk that we're going to get very emotional and say far too much. On the other hand, it could be that this eclipse helps us to detox a particular situation that's become very murky. Perhaps we have a change of perspective and are finally able to have a conversation that frees us from a situation that's been dragging us down.

If you're going through a rough time, please take heart.

> Although eclipse seasons can be very difficult if they hit you hard or if a lot of change is needed in your life, everything that happens at the time of an eclipse nearly always works out for the very best.

The eclipse is taking place in the sign of Taurus and communing with lucky Jupiter, as mentioned above. Pay extra attention to the 'How to Work with This Moon' section on the following page, because it could well be that this eclipse ignites the luck for you in whichever part of your chart is being activated by this Moon.

Gratitude at the Eclipse

With Jupiter being activated by this eclipse, it's a very good time to take a moment to think about what you're grateful for. Use the space below to list three people, places or things you know you're truly blessed to have in your life. If you have people on your list below, reach out and let them know.

1. _____

2. _____

3. _____

How to Work with This Moon

To discover where the energy of this Full Moon is for you, find your Star sign or Rising sign here, see which House is involved, and then read 'A Quick Guide to the Houses' (see page 25): Aries – 2nd House; Taurus – 1st House; Gemini – 12th House; Cancer – 11th House; Leo – 10th House; Virgo – 9th House; Libra – 8th House; Scorpio – 7th House; Sagittarius – 6th House; Capricorn – 5th House; Aquarius – 4th House; Pisces – 3rd House.

FULL MOON FORGIVENESS AND QUESTIONS TO ASK

One of the hardest things about Full Moon eclipses is that they require us to let go of someone or something and move on. Sometimes we're more than ready to let go, and sometimes we know we need to let go but we're just not emotionally ready yet. That's when eclipses can be the hardest. Forgive yourself if you've been misguidedly clinging on to something. Make a list of what you're releasing. Join me for a free Full Moon ritual via www.moonmessages.com/fbevents.

I forgive/release:

_____

_____

_____

_____

Where in my life do I need to let go and move on?

_____

Why have I been clinging on?

_____

What will letting go do for me?

_____

This Week

There's a Full Moon eclipse this week, so expect the energies to be edgy or even turbulent. Release your past, and anything that no longer serves you. Make that your aim this week.

23 October: the Sun moves into Scorpio

28/29 October: Full Moon eclipse occurs at 05°Ta09'

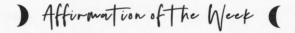 Affirmation of the Week

'I am willing to let go.'

Louise Hay

October – Week 43

23 Monday

♒ ◗

---

24 Tuesday

♒ ♓ ◗

---

25 Wednesday

♓ ◗

---

26 Thursday

♓ ♈ ◗

---

27 Friday

♈ ◯

---

28 Saturday

Full Moon eclipse: London: 21:24 | LA: 13:24 | New York: 16:24

♈ ♉ ◯

---

29 Sunday

Full Moon eclipse: Sydney: 07:24

♉ ◯

November

As November begins, we're out of the last eclipse season of 2023. How are you feeling? Did you manage to do some powerful energetic work while the eclipses were happening? Sometimes what life serves us up is hard to take – but the more we can lean into it, accept it and use it as a springboard for our personal growth, the better. If October was tough, November should be a salve.

As November begins, it's once again time to make 'Live and let live' our motto. This has been a big lesson for all of us, not just this year but over the past few years: sometimes we just have to cede control, and if we can do that in the first two weeks of November, it'll probably be a far less jarring experience. Overall, the energies are really quite pleasant.

However, although the energies in November are much calmer, there is a rather intense Mars clash with Uranus in the middle of the month. Just be careful how you go in the second week of the month – the energies then are going to be pretty intense, and some people might not be minding their own business or their p's and q's.

Then, at the end of the month, there are a couple of clashes with Saturn. In other words, there are more lessons coming our way. Saturn is telling us to pay attention, be a grown-up, be responsible and do what you said you were going to do. If someone's giving you a hard time towards the end of the month, give them a wide berth – but do be wise and mature.

> **This month I will:**
> ❑ Take my energetic 'medicine'
> ❑ Live and let live
> ❑ Be responsible

This Week

We're now out of the eclipse season and there is every reason to hope that life is going to be much easier to deal with! One issue related to love or abundance could turn around now.

31 October: festivals of Samhain (northern hemisphere) and Beltane (southern hemisphere)

4 November: Saturn retrograde ends

5 November: Third Quarter Moon

) What Are You Grateful For This Week? (

_____

_____

_____

_____

_____

October/November – Week 44

30 Monday

31 Tuesday

1 Wednesday

2 Thursday

3 Friday

4 Saturday

5 Sunday

Third Quarter Moon

This Week

This week brings some of the most intense energies of November. Meditate, meditate, meditate and you'll get through it all with flying colours! Also remember to breathe when stressed...

8 November: Venus moves into Libra

10 November: Mercury moves into Sagittarius

🌙 **What Are You Grateful For This Week?** 🌙

_____

_____

_____

_____

_____

November – Week 45

6 Monday

_____

7 Tuesday

_____

8 Wednesday

_____

9 Thursday

_____

10 Friday

_____

11 Saturday

_____

12 Sunday

_____

New Moon
in Scorpio

KEY WORDS AND IDEAS
FOR THIS LUNATION:

- Intense
- Competitive
- Snarky
- Electric

DATE AND TIME OF THIS MOON

London: 13 Nov, 09:27 | Sydney: 13 Nov, 20:27 | LA: 13 Nov, 01:27 | New York: 13 Nov, 04:27

Clearly, 2023 wants to go out with a bang not a whimper. Last month we had the eclipses and this month we have not another eclipse but a really electric New Moon.

For a start, the New Moon is taking place in the incredibly intense sign of Scorpio. (A little reminder that we all have Scorpio in our chart somewhere! That's just how astrology works. If you want to learn astrology, I have a course that you can start for free here: www.moonmessages.com/readmychart.)

Moreover, this New Moon is taking place right alongside the planet of fire, drive and determination, Mars. In ancient astrology, Mars actually rules the sign of Scorpio, so in a way, this is like having a match next to a fuse.

> **Expect life to be quite lively this month, especially in the lead-up to, and on the day of, the New Moon.**

But wait – there's more. Last but certainly not least is the fact that this New Moon is taking place in a really intense clash with the planet of chaos and craziness, Uranus. It truly is the icing on the cake.

On the one hand, this is an amazing New Moon to get yourself out of the doldrums, to shift your energy and to move on from being upset about anything or anyone. On the other hand, the energies really are a little bit out of control, so mind how you go.

When it comes utilizing these energies to make your New Moon wishes, one of the best things you can do for yourself is figure out what you need to liberate or free yourself from.

The Good Old Anti-Nonsense Method

This is a marvellous New Moon for anyone who needs to break free from limiting self-beliefs. One of my favourite techniques for breaking free is what I call the 'Good Old Anti-Nonsense Method'. To do this exercise, fill in the sentences below:

In the past, my limiting self-belief was that _____

_____

But that's nonsense! The truth is _____

_____

Realizing this, I am going to _____

_____

Continue on a separate piece of paper if you need more space than I've provided here. You can also find a PDF for this exercise in the 'Diary Bonuses' area at www.moonmessages.com/diarybonuses23.

How to Work with This Moon

To discover where the energy of this New Moon is for you, find your Star sign or Rising sign here, see which House is involved, and then read 'A Quick Guide to the Houses' (see page 25): Aries – 8th House; Taurus – 7th House; Gemini – 6th House; Cancer – 5th House; Leo – 4th House; Virgo – 3rd House; Libra – 2nd House; Scorpio – 1st House; Sagittarius – 12th House; Capricorn – 11th House; Aquarius – 10th House; Pisces – 9th House.

NEW MOON WISHES AND INTENTIONS

My current biggest, most audacious goal, wish or intention is:

_____

_____

Now turn it into an affirmation. Write it here as if it's already happened and keep repeating it until the Full Moon.

_____

_____

Action steps I'm going to take towards this goal:

In the next 24 hours

_____

In the coming week

_____

In the month ahead

_____

Tip: Write these actions you can take in the diary.

I commit to this goal whole-heartedly!

Sign here:

_____

This Week

The planet of challenges and lessons, Saturn, starts to go forwards again this week. In other words, it's time to do less rebuilding and more building of your life. But first there might be a few obstacles you need to surmount or get around.

13 November: New Moon occurs at 20°Sc43'

) Affirmation of the Week (

'Life supports me
in every possible way.'

LOUISE HAY

November — Week 46

13 Monday

New Moon: London: 09:27 | Sydney: 20:27 | LA: 01:27 | New York: 04:27

14 Tuesday

15 Wednesday

16 Thursday

17 Friday

18 Saturday

19 Sunday

This Week

Try not to worry if you say a bit too much or more than you meant to early this week. By the end of the week, it'll be relatively easy to have a healing conversation, if you're brave enough to have it.

20 November: First Quarter Moon

22 November: the Sun moves into Sagittarius

24 November: Mars moves into Sagittarius

🌙 What Are You Grateful For This Week? 🌙

_____

_____

_____

_____

_____

_____

November – Week 47

20 Monday

First Quarter Moon ♒ ♓ ◐

21 Tuesday

♓ ◐

22 Wednesday

♓ ♈ ◐

23 Thursday

♈ ◐

24 Friday

♈ ♉ ◐

25 Saturday

♉ ◐

26 Sunday

♉ ◐

Full Moon
in Gemini

KEY WORDS AND IDEAS
FOR THIS LUNATION:

- Interesting
- Confusing
- Mystical
- Angry

DATE AND TIME OF THIS MOON

London: 27 Nov, 09:16 | Sydney: 27 Nov, 20:16 | LA: 27 Nov, 01:16 | New York: 27 Nov, 04:16

On paper, this Full Moon looks fairly straightforward. It's in the sign of Gemini and not making any immediate alignments with any planets.

However, when you look at the situation a little more closely, it becomes apparent that in fact the Gemini planet Mercury is in a bit of a mess this week! It's making a hard angle to the planet of confusion and deception, Neptune. Added to the regular heightened emotions that come with pretty much every Full Moon is the fact that many of us are just not going to know which way is up!

To find out where you're going to be experiencing all this, as always, check out the 'How to Work with This Moon' section. The House that's being activated is where it's possible you're going to either turn the corner or really not be sure of which direction to head in at all!

Adding celestial fuel to the cosmic fire, as the Full Moon takes place we also have Mars, the planet of anger and determination, testosterone and war, aligning with the Sun. It really is a pretty combustible combination. Angry words are likely to be heard!

If you know you have a short fuse at the best of times, up your meditation practice and deep breathing this week. Also remember that everything happens for a reason!

Cooling the Fire Meditation

This month, for something different, I'd like to offer you this 'Cooling the Fire' meditation. Sometimes fire is great because it fires us up. And sometimes it burns! This meditation should help you to make the best of it without getting singed! Just hold your phone camera over the QR code below to access the meditation, or visit www.moonmessages.com/cooling.

How to Work with This Moon

To discover where the energy of this Full Moon is for you, find your Star sign or Rising sign here, see which House is involved, and then read 'A Quick Guide to the Houses' (see page 25): Aries – 3rd House; Taurus – 2nd House; Gemini – 1st House; Cancer – 12th House; Leo – 11th House; Virgo – 10th House; Libra – 9th House; Scorpio – 8th House; Sagittarius – 7th House; Capricorn – 6th House; Aquarius – 5th House; Pisces – 4th House.

FULL MOON FORGIVENESS
AND QUESTIONS TO ASK

One of the reasons we practise forgiveness and release at the time of the Full Moon is that this is when we experience our feelings most strongly. Rather than suppressing those feelings with alcohol, food or whatever else you can think of, process them instead. What do you need to make peace with and release? Join me for a free Full Moon ritual via www.moonmessages.com/fbevents.

I forgive/release:

_____

_____

_____

_____

What am I still really angry about from my past?

_____

Can I understand that letting go of the anger doesn't make what happened okay but frees me from the past?

_____

On that basis, am I willing to let this anger go?

_____

This Week

After a few up-and-down alignments, finally this week we have a lovely, steady Mercury–Saturn connection that's going to augur well for decent conversations and for agreements that stick.

27 November: Full Moon occurs at 04°Ge51'

1 December: Mercury moves into Capricorn

❯ Affirmation of the Week ❮

'I forgive myself
for not being perfect.'

LOUISE HAY

November/December – Week 48

27 Monday

Full Moon: London: 09:16 | Sydney: 20:16 | LA: 01:16 | New York: 04:16 ♉♊◯

28 Tuesday

♊◯

29 Wednesday

♊♋◯

30 Thursday

♋◗

1 Friday

♋♌◗

2 Saturday

♌◗

3 Sunday

♌◗

December

Third Quarter Moon: 5 December
New Moon: 12/13 December
First Quarter Moon: 19 December
Full Moon: 26/27 December

So here we are, wrapping up 2023. Just as with the past few months, hopefully December will be relatively smooth sailing, without any major dramas. Certainly there are no major planetary alignments happening in this last month of the year.

Rather, what we have as we move towards the end of 2023 is the end of Mercury retrograde and great energies for conversations about important matters, clearing up confusion, more healing, romance and even scope for obsessive love relationships.

As you move through December, spend a little time filling out the Farewell and Welcome Exercise (*see pages 272–275*). How do you feel about the year that was? What were the highs and the lows? What upsets do you still need to release? What are you looking forward to in 2024?

Mid-month, the planet of communications, Mercury, will shake things up one last time for the year and go into a retrograde cycle that will last through to 2024. It'll bring with it second chances and opportunities to make great end-of-year deals, one way or another.

The period between Christmas and New Year is marked by some rather confusing Neptune alignments, so go easy on the good cheer if you don't want to end up with a sore head!

My hope that is 2023 has been a pretty good year for you, and another step in the right direction for humanity. I also hope dearly that this diary has helped you remember how powerful you really are, and that you'll continue to work with the Moon.

This month I will:
- ❏ Have a healing conversation
- ❏ Drop past regrets
- ❏ Embrace romance!

This Week

A week that should go well — there are no nasty planetary alignments — so going by the 'as above, so below' theory on which astrology is founded, hopefully all will be well in your world.

4 December: Venus moves into Scorpio

5 December: Third Quarter Moon

6 December: Neptune retrograde ends

❯ What Are You Grateful For This Week? ❮

December – Week 49

4 Monday

♌ ♍ ◐

5 Tuesday

Third Quarter Moon ♍ ◐

6 Wednesday

♍ ♎ ◐

7 Thursday

♎ ◐

8 Friday

♎ ◐

9 Saturday

♎ ♏ ◐

10 Sunday

♏ ◐

New Moon in Sagittarius

KEY WORDS AND IDEAS FOR THIS LUNATION:

- Healing
- Confusing
- See the funny side
- See the bigger picture

DATE AND TIME OF THIS MOON
London: 12 Dec, 23:32 | Sydney: 13 Dec, 10:32 | LA: 12 Dec, 15:32 | New York: 12 Dec, 18:32

The first thing to say about the New Moon in Sagittarius is that it's always a chance to step back and look at the bigger picture of life. So often we humans bury ourselves in the details, thinking only about our own worries and not looking around us to see the bigger picture of where we are in life. Taking a bit of a step back and getting some perspective helps us to see we are in fact blessed.

That said, this New Moon does have a slightly confusing aspect to it. Like the Gemini New Moon earlier this year (Gemini being the sign opposite Sagittarius), this New Moon is clashing with Neptune, the planet of confusion and deception (among other things – Neptune does also have a very positive side!).

Think back to six months ago. Was there a situation that you found confusing? Was there a deception? It could well be there is some kind of fallout coming now – or, with any luck, a conclusion or closure!

The planet Mars is harmonizing with the healing planetoid Chiron under this New Moon. So we could all really benefit from some kind of spiritual physical activity – yoga, tai chi or chi kung, or even just being more proactive about meditating, or whatever practice works for you.

A Spooky Sports Challenge

Here's a challenge for you. To honour the energies around this New Moon, commit to doing a little bit of exercise every day between now and the Full Moon. (I'll do it too!) Just do whatever you're capable of. It could be 'chair yoga' (which you can find online) or daily Sun Salutations or, if you know chi kung or tai chi, do that.

I've also created a special 'shaking' video for you, which anyone can do with no training at all, in the 'Diary Bonuses' area at www.moonmessages.com/diarybonuses2023. Try it for 14 days – it'll change your life in amazing ways!

How to Work with This Moon

To discover where the energy of this New Moon is for you, find your Star sign or Rising sign here, see which House is involved, and then read 'A Quick Guide to the Houses' (see page 25): Aries – 9th House; Taurus – 8th House; Gemini – 7th House; Cancer – 6th House;

Leo – 5th House; Virgo – 4th House; Libra – 3rd House; Scorpio – 12th House; Sagittarius – 1st House; Capricorn – 12th House; Aquarius – 11th House; Pisces – 10th House.

NEW MOON WISHES AND INTENTIONS

My current biggest, most audacious goal, wish or intention is:

_____

_____

Now turn it into an affirmation. Write it here as if it's already happened and keep repeating it until the Full Moon.

_____

_____

Action steps I'm going to take towards this goal:

In the next 24 hours

_____

In the coming week

_____

In the month ahead

_____

Tip: Write these actions you can take in the diary.

I commit to this goal whole-heartedly!

Sign here:

_____

This Week

This week has some lovely astrology and some confusing energies as well. Focus on the good stuff and just trust that any strange weirdness will pass soon enough – because it will.

12/13 December: New Moon occurs at 20°Sg40'

13 December: Mercury goes retrograde (until 1 January 2024)

❯ Affirmation of the Week ❮

'I am healthy, whole,
and complete.'

LOUISE HAY

December – Week 50

11 Monday

♏ ↗ ♐ ⬤

12 Tuesday

New Moon: London: 23:32 | LA: 15:32 | New York: 18:32   ♐ ⬤

13 Wednesday

New Moon: Sydney: 10:32   ♐ ♑ ⬤

14 Thursday

♑ ⬤

15 Friday

♑ ♒ ⬤

16 Saturday

♒ ⬤

17 Sunday

♒ ♓ ◖

This Week

For those of us who celebrate Christmas Day, Hanukkah, Winter/Summer Solstice or any other holidays around this time, the good news is that the energies are looking pretty darned friendly. May we all rejoice and be glad.

19 December: First Quarter Moon

22 December: the Sun moves into Capricorn, marking the fourth and final Cardinal ingress of the year. Check into the Diary Bonuses area (www.moonmessages.com/diarybonuses2023) for your 'Reflect and Review' worksheet

22 December: Winter Solstice/Yule (northern hemisphere) and Summer Solstice/Litha (southern hemisphere)

23 December: Mercury moves into Sagittarius

 **What Are You Grateful For This Week?**

December – Week 51

18 Monday

♓ ◐

19 Tuesday

First Quarter Moon

♓ ♈ ◐

20 Wednesday

♈ ◐

21 Thursday

♈ ◐

22 Friday

◐ ♈ ♉ ○

23 Saturday

♉ ○

24 Sunday

○ ♉ ♊ ○

Full Moon in Cancer

KEY WORDS AND IDEAS FOR THIS LUNATION:

- Confusing (again)
- Homely
- Seeking a work–life balance
- Forthright

DATE AND TIME OF THIS MOON

London: 27 Dec, 00:33 | Sydney: 27 Dec, 11:33 | LA: 26 Dec, 16:33 | New York: 26 Dec, 19:33

Sometimes it seems as though there is a theme in the air with the planets. Right now that theme seems to be confusion! Reason being, not only is the planet of communications, Mercury, going backwards, but as it does so, it's repeating a clash with the planet of confusion, Neptune.

> **As we celebrate the last Full Moon of the year, there are going to be some people feeling as though they're just not sure which way is up!**

Actually, since Neptune also rules alcohol, it could just be that a lot of people are drinking too much! That's probably a reasonable assumption at this time of year, but don't take it too far.

In case this all sounds a little bit ominous, I'd also like to mention here the good news that 2024 has some pretty good astrology ahead. In other words, even if the end of this year is a little bit weird in some way for you, keep your mind focused on the fact that it's nearly the new year. Even though I always like to remind you that calendars are just a man-made construct, there's no doubt that the end of one year and the start of a new one is a very good time to set new intentions.

So even though it's a Full Moon, don't just think about what you're moving on from; keep one eye on your aims for the year ahead.

The Grandmama of 2023 Release Ceremonies

One thing I've really tried to encourage you to do this year is to use every single Full Moon to forgive and release and move on. So maybe you feel like you've been doing this all year, and indeed I hope you *do* feel that way. But this is the grandmama of them all —the last Full Moon of the year — so your exercise now is to put everything you have into the year's final Forgiveness and Release list (*opposite*). Spend time with it, feel it deep down, and then burn that piece of paper! Just release anything and everything from 2023 that you want to move on from.

How to Work with This Moon

To discover where the energy of this Full Moon is for you, find your Star sign or Rising sign here, see which House is involved, and then read 'A Quick Guide to the Houses' (*see page 25*): Aries – 4th House; Taurus – 3rd House; Gemini – 2nd House; Cancer – 1st House; Leo – 12th House; Virgo – 11th House; Libra – 10th House; Scorpio – 9th House; Sagittarius – 8th House; Capricorn – 7th House; Aquarius – 6th House; Pisces – 5th House.

FULL MOON FORGIVENESS
AND QUESTIONS TO ASK

This is it: your chance to release and let go of anything and everything in your life — from the past month, the past year, from forever! Every Full Moon is an important time to tap into this process, but the last Full Moon of the year in the emotional sign of Cancer is ideal. Let it go! Join me for a free Full Moon ritual via www.moonmessages.com/fbevents.

I forgive/release:

_____

_____

_____

What am I grateful for this month?

_____

_____

What am I releasing from this month?

_____

_____

What do I want more of in January 2024?

_____

_____

This Week

Overall, this week — which is a celebration for many around the world, one way or another — looks pretty positive. There's just still some scope for more of that confusion that keeps swirling around us right now!

26/27 December: Full Moon occurs at 04°Cn58'

29 December: Venus moves into Sagittarius

31 December: Jupiter retrograde ends

) Affirmation of the Week (

'The past is over and done and has no power over me. I can begin to be free in this moment.'

Louise Hay

December – Week 52

25 Monday

♊ ○

26 Tuesday

Full Moon: LA: 16:33 | New York: 19:33

♊ ♋ ○

27 Wednesday

Full Moon: London: 00:33 | Sydney: 11:33

♋ ○

28 Thursday

♋ ○

29 Friday

♋ ♌ ○

30 Saturday

♌ ○

31 Sunday

♌ ♍ ○

Farewell and Welcome Exercise

For many years, I've been encouraging readers of my various columns to do a short exercise at the end of every year. This year, I wanted to include it in this diary.

The idea is a simple one. At the end of every year it's important to reflect on what's been, and take a moment to consider the highs and the lows, the challenges and the opportunities. Most importantly, it's a chance to bid farewell to what didn't work for you, to be grateful for what did, and to start hatching some ideas for the year ahead.

So, thinking back over 2023, what are you leaving behind? Think about any dramas or upsets you experienced, clashes you may have had with family, friends or colleagues, any fears you went through and any low points. Also think about the things you're happy to leave behind. Write them all down on the opposite page, then rip it out and burn it!

And then? It's time to welcome in 2024! What do you want to attract into your life? Take a moment to think about what you're grateful for in your life and what you want to attract into your life in the coming 12 months.

WHAT AM I LEAVING BEHIND FROM 2023?

I forgive everyone
in my life for all
perceived wrongs.
I release them
with love.

LOUISE HAY

WHAT DO I WANT TO WELCOME IN 2024?

_____

_____

_____

_____

_____

_____

_____

_____

_____

_____

_____

_____

_____

_____

_____

_____

_____

_____

_____

_____

This Week

Don't judge 2024 by 1 January! There are some tough energies around, but the year ahead looks pretty good overall.

1 January: Mercury retrograde ends

4 January: Third Quarter Moon

☽ What Are You Grateful For This Week? ☾

January 2024 – Week 1

1 Monday

♍︎ ◐

2 Tuesday

♍︎ ◐

3 Wednesday

♍︎ ♎︎ ◐

4 Thursday

Third Quarter Moon

♎︎ ◐

5 Friday

♎︎ ♏︎ ◐

6 Saturday

♏︎ ◐

7 Sunday

♏︎ ♐︎ ◐

JANUARY

M	T	W	T	F	S	S
1	2	3	4	5	6	7
8	9	10	11	12	13	14
15	16	17	18	19	20	21
22	23	24	25	26	27	28
29	30	31				

FEBRUARY

M	T	W	T	F	S	S
			1	2	3	4
5	6	7	8	9	10	11
12	13	14	15	16	17	18
19	20	21	22	23	24	25
26	27	28	29			

MARCH

M	T	W	T	F	S	S
				1	2	3
4	5	6	7	8	9	10
11	12	13	14	15	16	17
18	19	20	21	22	23	24
25	26	27	28	29	30	31

APRIL

M	T	W	T	F	S	S
1	2	3	4	5	6	7
8	9	10	11	12	13	14
15	16	17	18	19	20	21
22	23	24	25	26	27	28
29	30					

MAY

M	T	W	T	F	S	S
		1	2	3	4	5
6	7	8	9	10	11	12
13	14	15	16	17	18	19
20	21	22	23	24	25	26
27	28	29	30	31		

JUNE

M	T	W	T	F	S	S
					1	2
3	4	5	6	7	8	9
10	11	12	13	14	15	16
17	18	19	20	21	22	23
24	25	26	27	28	29	30

JULY

M	T	W	T	F	S	S
1	2	3	4	5	6	7
8	9	10	11	12	13	14
15	16	17	18	19	20	21
22	23	24	25	26	27	28
29	30	31				

AUGUST

M	T	W	T	F	S	S
			1	2	3	4
5	6	7	8	9	10	11
12	13	14	15	16	17	18
19	20	21	22	23	24	25
26	27	28	29	30	31	

SEPTEMBER

M	T	W	T	F	S	S
						1
2	3	4	5	6	7	8
9	10	11	12	13	14	15
16	17	18	19	20	21	22
23	24	25	26	27	28	29
30						

OCTOBER

M	T	W	T	F	S	S
	1	2	3	4	5	6
7	8	9	10	11	12	13
14	15	16	17	18	19	20
21	22	23	24	25	26	27
28	29	30	31			

NOVEMBER

M	T	W	T	F	S	S
			1	2	3	
4	5	6	7	8	9	10
11	12	13	14	15	16	17
18	19	20	21	22	23	24
25	26	27	28	29	30	

DECEMBER

M	T	W	T	F	S	S
						1
2	3	4	5	6	7	8
9	10	11	12	13	14	15
16	17	18	19	20	21	22
23	24	25	26	27	28	29
30	31					

Notes

Also by Yasmin Boland

Discover how to work with the magical energies of the Moon to manifest positive change and create the life of your dreams!

Moonology™ Oracle Cards
A 44-Card Deck and Guidebook
978-1-78180-996-9

Moonology™ Manifestation Oracle Cards
A 48-Card Deck and Guidebook
978-1-78817-652-1

About the Author

Award-winning astrologer and *Sunday Times* bestselling author Yasmin Boland was born in Germany to English/Irish/Maltese parents and grew up in Hobart, Tasmania. After university, she worked as a newspaper journalist, which led her from Tasmania to 'mainland' Australia and eventually to London, where she worked as a journalist and a radio and TV producer.

In the 1990s, learning how to meditate completely changed Yasmin's life, also opening her up to astrology. Her passion for astrology eventually became her profession, and Yasmin is now one of the most widely read astrology writers on the planet. Yasmin loves all astrology but has a special interest in the Moon.

In 2022, Yasmin was voted one of the 100 Most Spiritually Influential Living People.

Yasmin is the bestselling author of *Moonology*™, *Astrology Made Easy*, *The Mercury Retrograde Book*, *Moonology*™ *Oracle Cards* and *Moonology*™ *Manifestation Oracle Cards*.

- yasminboland
- @yasminboland
- @moonologydotcom and @planetyasminboland
- www.yasminboland.com and www.moonology.com